REBUILDING AMERICA

REBUILDING AMERICA

The Case for
Economic Regulation

Frederick C. Thayer

PRAEGER

PRAEGER SPECIAL STUDIES • PRAEGER SCIENTIFIC

New York • Philadelphia • Eastbourne, UK
Toronto • Hong Kong • Tokyo • Sydney

Library of Congress Cataloging in Publication Data

Thayer, Frederick C.
  Rebuilding America.

  1. Trade regulation—United States.   I. Title.
HD3616.U47T43 1984   338.973   83-17789
ISBN 0-03-061745-6 (alk. paper)

Published in 1984 by Praeger Publishers
CBS Educational and Professional Publishing
a Division of CBS Inc.
521 Fifth Avenue, New York, NY 10175 USA

© 1984 by Praeger Publishers

456789 052 98765432

Printed in the United States of America
on acid-free paper

Introduction

The May 30, 1983, edition of *Newsweek* had this question emblazoned on its cover: *"Can the Recovery Last?"* The headline appeared just after some economic indicators had signaled for a few months that the longest and deepest U.S. economic slump since World War II might be coming to an end. Headline writers, economic gurus, and policy-makers may be forgiven for proclaiming that the "recovery" had arrived, because optimism always sells better than pessimism. But it might have been appropriate to delay the proclamations until a significant number of jobless citizens had returned to work. Admitting that my answer is unlikely to be immediately popular, I suggest that while minor upturns in indicators may occasionally make it appear that things are getting better, anything properly labeled "recovery" is wholly impossible without a massive change in what Americans (and others) believe about market systems, and without tackling head-on the global crisis of industrial overcapacity and/or overproduction that threatens to make the current depression an endless one.

I will refer much more often in this book to economic "depressions" than to "recessions," because I have concluded that the latter term is used in inadvertently misleading ways that have the effect of reinforcing indefensible precepts of economic theory. The word "recession" is something of a corollary to the notion of "business cycles" that, as economists would have it, fluctuate around the presumably normal and desired state of equilibrium. The plotting of economic cycles has led in the past to some rather exotic formulations, among them the idea that business cycles are determined by sun spots (if these affect weather and, therefore, agriculture, a possibility), and the idea that the most important cycles occur in "long waves" (by implication, beyond human control). In the contemporary world of economics, a wholly insignificant change in economic indicators immediately is labeled as either the beginning or end of a recession.

The National Bureau of Economic Research, a private, nonprofit group of American economists, whose views on such matters are widely accepted, decided on July 7, 1983, that the most recent recession, having begun in July, 1981, had come to an end in November, 1982, at a time when unemployment in the United States was hovering about the 10 percent level. The same organization, recapitulating the eleven most recent U.S. recessions, declared that the downturn which had begun in August, 1929, had ended in March, 1933, the next recession having lasted from May, 1937, to June, 1938.[1] Those who have read about, or experienced, the Great Depression of the 1930s might dispute such a declaration. Are the 1930s best described as a decade of general prosperity, interrupted only occasionally by recessions, or as a period of prolonged depression and misery, affected hardly at all by two inconsequential recoveries? Those who label 1933 as a year of economic recovery might not be the appropriate authorities for so designating 1983.

I take "depression," an economic phenomenon that has yet to be given a precise technical definition, to be very nearly as applicable to the economic world of the 1980s as it was to the 1930s. From the perspective argued in this book, the widely proclaimed "recovery" of 1983 cannot, as things stand now, lead to the sustained "boom" that some observers see immediately ahead. While "recession" does indeed come fully equipped with a precise definition, it is a wholly misleading one. As was the case in 1933 and 1938, a declaration that "recovery has arrived" turns the heads of policy-makers away from problems they might otherwise be prepared to face — because the problems are large, they call for equally large solutions.

The task ahead encompasses the dual objectives of reorganizing and rebuilding America, neither having anything in common with such contemporary slogans as "reindustrialization," "become more competitive," and "move to the high-tech frontier." The slogans merely reflect an obsession with producing things to sell — an obsession unique neither to America nor to capitalists, and one which offers little hope at a time when American and world markets are overstuffed with plants that cannot be used and goods that cannot be sold for the costs of making them. To understand the two inseparable dimensions of the task, it is first necessary to sweep aside the economic theories that bring only ruin — a charge from which no school of economic thought is exempt. One requirement is to reorganize industry across the board, in America and perhaps in the rest of the world as well, so as to check the runaway and destructive forces of unrestrained competition. The second requirement is to rebuild the public works structure that now crumbles before our eyes. Contrary to the popular view, which most Americans have learned at the feet of economists, the need is for less private sector spending and more public sector spending – a perspective which is at odds with all versions of economic theory. The great failure of Keynesianism, for example, was that it emphasized only the latter, a disastrously unbalanced approach. My own efforts to unravel the presumably unchallengeable verities of economics began with the study of airline regulation.

As one who had long argued that the airline industry should be treated as a public utility and regulated accordingly, I found that those committed to classical economic doctrines refuse to take seriously any argument that a particular industry, the airlines in this case, requires or deserves special treatment. Acknowledging the drawbacks of any argument that gives the appearance of a vested interest, even though I have had no connection with the industry, I searched diligently for an unassailable argument in favor of airline regulation. What I found instead was that the industry was indeed not very unique (economists would agree), but that this industry and all other industries must be economically regulated in some fashion if they are to remain viable (economists would vehemently disagree). As I now see it, there can be no exception to this general proposition.

Nobody can argue for economic regulation across the board without dealing with the fundamental propositions of classical economic theory. I refer to microeconomics, the study of the behavior of individual buyers and sellers in (more or less) free or perfect markets. As a student of organizational behavior and decision-making, dissecting those propositions did not take me into wholly unfamiliar territory, in that the accepted designs for rational decision-making are drawn from microeconomics. I found it impossible to avoid the conclusion that a free market cannot, under any circumstances, tend toward or approach any form of equilibrium, but must inevitably slide into a depression. The propositions of classical economic theory (as much a theology as a theory) are easily understood, and are wholly incorrect. Adam Smith and those who followed his lead sought to minimize or remove the repressive authority of centralized monopolies. With the best of intentions, they constructed an indefensible mythology that, in operation, has produced only one economic disaster after another.

As the time approaches for another quadrennial exercise in electing a U.S. president, I think it important to suggest that the toughest issues facing us all are not those which are in dispute among political parties, ideologies, and economists, but are, rather, the by-products of widespread agreement. This agreement extends well beyond the boundaries of this country, and the parties to the agreement unwittingly are pushing the world over an economic cliff. Disagreements, even when they become the issues of presidential campaigns, concern relatively trivial matters. Because all current proposals for U.S. economic recovery, liberal or conservative, seek to reduce government borrowing and spending in favor of increased private sector borrowing and spending, the adoption of any or all of the proposals can only deepen the depression.

That economists of all persuasions agree on most of the fundamentals of classical doctrine is easily demonstrated. In a recent book, Lester Thurow questions the assumptions of "price-auction" economics – his label for classical dogma – acknowledging that such schools of thought as monetarism, supply-side economics, and rational expectations all depend upon those assumptions. He errs, I think, in asserting that Keynesianism "replaced" classical doctrine during the Great Depression, and also "rescued economics" and society while it did so.[2] Since Thurow is a Keynesian, it is understandable that he would largely exempt Keynesianism from his challenge. If it "rescued economics" for a time, this is because it was wholly in conformance with classical principles, and so I shall argue.

From a different perspective, Young America's Foundation recently published a collection of essays providing a free market critique of the dominant economic textbooks now used in American colleges and universities. Former Treasury Secretary William E. Simon, writing the foreword for the collection, proclaims that it is time to discard the "failed and broken dogmas of Keynesian orthodoxy" by adopting the views of such "great economists" as Milton Friedman and Friedrich Hayek. One of the book's authors acknowledges immediately, however, that even in the most Keynesian of texts, there is much "valuable economic analysis upon which there is no important disagreement among economists."[3] The volume errs, I think, in excluding Keynesianism from the rank of classical theories.

Within the discipline, then, liberals often assert that Keynesianism remains valid while other schools of thought are invalid, while conservatives reverse the argument. My conclusion moves one further step; because Keynes did not depart from the fundamentals of classical doctrine, his theory and all the other prominent schools of thought differ only on macroeconomic behavior, issues, and policies. Briefly, macroeconomics deals with aggregates (all buyers and all sellers, and budgetary and monetary policies that presumably affect those aggregates). As I shall argue, all schools of economic thought assume that overcapacity and overproduction are essentially impossible or at least insignificant. However, these outcomes are absolutely inevitable in free markets. Underconsumption, in the Keynesian sense (insufficient demand for what is produced), is by no means the same as overproduction.

There was a time when large-scale overcapacity, overproduction, and depression could be defined as problems of capitalism, if only because the industrial revolution and privately owned enterprises emerged before socialism became an ostensibly rival doctrine. Marxists today cling to the incorrect position that ownership makes a difference, but it cannot. The problem always has been the unrestricted and unregulated competition among the many producers who seek to sell to the same customers. Today, more than ever, the competition is global, and competitors cannot be identified by a single political or economic ideology. Whatever their ideologies, all the competitors, whether farmers, firms, or countries, are victims of the same philosophy. Unregulated competition, within societies or in the world at large, remains the only cause of depression. This is best understood if markets are visualized as organizations.

If only regulation of market entry, output, and, perhaps, prices can prevent depression, or make recovery possible, this need not always, or even most of the time, require direct government involvement in the detailed decision-making processes of industry. This book defends economic regulation but not all regulatory agencies, many of which have been prevented from doing a good job. While it may be immediately important to reregulate some industries recently deregulated in this country — all of them casualties of classical theory — and while some government involvement would be necessary in order to reorganize those industries, the ultimate problem is a much larger one. If global free competition leads only to global depression and/or war, then only global regulation of supply can provide a solution.

Indeed, regulation of supply would make much less necessary the clumsy forms of government intervention that now find favor among various schools of economic thought. Keynesians, for example, believe that government regulation (stimulation) of demand often is needed, while the monetarists hold that government regulation of the money supply is the answer. These proposals, and many others, merely seek to perpetuate classical theory by ignoring the obvious problem of overproduction. Because socialism and capitalism, moreover, are only minor variants of the philosophy that overproduction is impossible, neither provides a solution.

I briefly outline below what I take to be some of the more unusual propositions argued in this book:

- During the final years of Herbert Hoover's presidency and the early years of Franklin Roosevelt's tenure, there was more agreement than disagreement about the causes of, and the solutions for, a depression. This has been forgotten because the study of economics has taken precedence over the study of history. Thurow is correct in observing that "economists could not agree then on what caused the Depression or what to do to get out of it"[4] — wholly understandable because economists perceive depressions only as aberrations that cannot be explained by a theory based upon perfection. The historians' analyses of recurring depressions stand up now, as do the agreements of the early 1930s (which were not Keynesian and did not include economists). "Overproduction" was then a staple of political vocabularies.

- Wartime U.S. prosperity was not traceable to Keynesianism, but to the regulation of supply caused by a large-scale diversion to military production. Postwar prosperity resulted from a unique form of regulation that has yet to be understood. Much of the world's industrial capacity was destroyed by military action. This had the effect of restricting competition after the war, thereby ensuring American prosperity for many years. If future large-scale wars must be nuclear ones, a substitute for this "regulation by war" is urgently needed.

- While antitrust laws constitute a long-term policy failure, they inadvertently contributed to postwar prosperity. Each of the most dominant firms in many industries feared that if it competed as vigorously as possible for customers, its success might incite the Department of Justice to take antitrust action. This important and largely invisible form of economic regulation did much to prevent overcapacity and overproduction.

• When other forms of economic regulation are not feasible, firms often decide they must collude or conspire in order to avoid the ravages of unbridled competition. In this sense, antitrust laws have the unintended effect of creating criminals. What is now labeled "illegal collusion" should be transformed into "legalized planning."

• The double-bookkeeping fallacies of classical economics have made a shambles of U.S. policy-making. Unneeded industrial plants are built because they mistakenly are defined as "wealth," even when their output cannot be sold. Meanwhile, we avoid building public works because they are just as mistakenly labeled "waste," even when badly needed. Contrary to what double-bookkeeping tells us, government borrowing and spending are much less of a problem than borrowing and spending for unneeded industrial plants. Americans describe the latter as "private-sector investment" but, in much of the rest of the world, governments keep better books while making the same mistakes we do. They also overbuild plant capacity, because they must borrow according to our rules.

• Contemporary liberals correctly support effective social regulation of safety and health standards, but fail to see that the economic regulation they oppose is an indispensable prerequisite for the former. Contemporary conservatives correctly complain that social regulation makes them less competitive, by imposing additional costs, but fail to see that economic regulation would remove the reason for their opposition to the former.

• Horizontal mergers (within an industry) can be helpful in rationalizing and otherwise regulating production. A conglomerate merger (the purchase of one firm by another in a different industry) only intensifies competition and leads to further deterioration in general economic conditions. Current policy, unfortunately, is more favorable to the latter than to the former.

I do not present in this book a detailed justification for a huge public works program. The evidence can easily be located in the references cited in Chapter 7, at least for this country. Citizens of many countries are well aware that streets, roads, highways, bridges, public transportation, and sewer and water systems are in deplorable states of disrepair. In countries which have had high rates of industrial activity for some time, many other problems demand attention — among them, chemical dumps. My targets are the economic theories and bookkeeping practices that lead policy makers, often with widespread voter support in countries that hold elections, to believe they will be guilty of economic crimes if they spend anything more than token amounts on such undertakings. Americans especially tend to define freedom as the ability to shop at well-stocked department stores. Indeed, when the American hostages in Iran were released in 1981, their first scheduled activity, after a physical checkup, was a reintroduction to freedom in the form of a visit to a large military department store temporarily closed to other patrons. Despite what economic theories claim to be impossible, it is indeed possible to have too many stores and too many goods; worse than that, it is the inevitable outcome of an unrestrained market. Meanwhile, we approach a time when the roads leading to the stores will be impassable. The supreme irony is that overspending on public works, while it ought not be done lightly, cannot ruin an economy to the same extent as overspending on industrial plants. A shift from private- to public-sector spending, moreover, need not involve "tax" increases, provided the word is correctly defined. Billions in hidden taxes (labeled "prices") now go into unneeded plant capacity and merger wars.

This book admittedly violates the academic good manners customarily expected of an author who crosses over from his own discipline to another. As one trained in political science (public administration and international politics), I should use an interdisciplinary approach by applying the accepted concepts and techniques of economics to policy problems that engage my interest. Because I challenge the fundamental propositions of economics, I doubtless will offend some readers trained in that discipline. While this critique of economics moves beyond my earlier one, I can only note that I have raised equally serious questions about theories of politics and administration.[5]

Some of the material in Chapters 4 and 5 has appeared in somewhat different form in articles published in the *Journal of Public and International Affairs, The Logistics and Transportation Review,* and *The American University Law Review.*[6] I thank the journals for permission to draw from those works.

NOTES

1. *New York Times*, July 9, 1983, p. 17.

2. Lester C. Thurow, *Dangerous Currents: The State of Economics* (New York: Random House, 1983), pp. xv, xviii.

3. Craig Bolton et al., eds., *American Economics Texts: A Critique* (Reston, Va.: Young America's Foundation, 1982), pp. ix, 3.

4. Thurow, op. cit., p. xv.

5. See my *An End to Hierarchy & Competition: Administration in the Post-Affluent World* (New York and London: Franklin Watts New Viewpoints, 2d ed. 1981).

6. "Competitive Bidding and Public Administration: The Unhappy Marriage," *Journal of Public and International Affairs* 2, 2 (Spring/Summer 1981): 137-50; "Airline Regulation: The Case for a Public Utility Approach," *The Logistics and Transportation Review* 18, 3 (1981): 211-34; "Regulation Is Inevitable: Legal Planning or Illegal Collusion?," *The American University Law Review* 32 (Winter 1983): 425-53.

Table of Contents

REBUILDING AMERICA

1
Economics:
Fundamentals, Origins, and Devices

Given the prominence of economics, especially as a discipline widely taught in universities and colleges, it would appear, at first glance, wholly inappropriate to begin by outlining its basic fundamentals. From the perspective advanced in this book, however, economics is a form of doublespeak in which black is made white, the evil is made good, and, above all, the grossly inefficient and wasteful is somehow labeled efficient and frugal. If the idealized free market of perfect competition can lead only to a deep economic depression and to social chaos, it follows that economic theory must obscure more than it explains; and so I argue. The more effort that goes into peeling away the layers of obscurity, the less there is to be found underneath them. The theory and the discipline have been trying for two centuries, and with considerable success, to convince us all that somehow or other, free markets can rescue us from the oppressive centralized authority of monopoly producers, public or private. This success, which has had the effect of preserving the theory and discipline at a considerable cost to the societies presumably served, has been achieved only by ignoring the simple and most fundamental characteristics of free-market competition. Were this not the case, this country and others might have been able to avoid the periodic economic slumps that have marked modern economic history.

As I repeatedly mumbled about the preposterous basis of economic thought, I had the good fortune to have as a colleague a well-trained historian (Donald Goldstein) who, listening to such words

1

as "overproduction" and "overexpansion," reminded me several times that whatever economists might say about depressions (in recent times, the most popular explanation, attributable to John Maynard Keynes, is a "deficiency" or "collapse" in demand), historians repeatedly had used the same terms as I used. In stripping economics to its basics, I will begin there, after making a needed clarification.

While "overproduction" is an acceptable description of the inevitable outcomes of unregulated competition, neither Marx nor his followers, who used the word to criticize capitalism, fully understood the problem. In the preface to the 1888 English translation of the Communist manifesto, Engels referred to the "powers of the nether world" that bourgeois society, once having unleashed, could not "control." These "powers," he asserted, created the recurring "epidemic" of overproduction. Marx believed that in a competitive market, price would be determined primarily by the amount of labor time used in production (this was an incorrect assumption, but one wholly compatible with classical equilibrium theory); in a free market, as I shall argue, price is determined by the degree of competition, and nothing prevents price from falling well below costs of production. The more contemporary Marxist view is that because less is produced than is needed to meet even the minimum health needs of all people, the problem is more "a lack of purchasing power" than overproduction; this view is compatible with much of Keynesian economics.[1] Action to increase purchasing power may indeed be necessary, but it cannot be sufficient. Marxists, then, share not only with Keynesians, but with all other schools of economic thought, the widespread lack of understanding about how competition must function, in one society or in the world.

THE BARE BONES OF ECONOMICS

Writing in 1959, a prominent historian in this country looked back upon the 1893 "panic" — a word that later gave way to "depression" as the label for an economic slump:

In retrospect it is possible to distinguish a number of deeper causes of the depression. In the first place, many industries, in particular the railroads, had expanded their activities far beyond the market demand. During the 1880's almost 74,000 miles of railroad were built, more than during any previous decade. Much of this expansion was dictated not by any reasonable estimate of traffic possibilities but by the pressure of competition; each road recklessly and hastily threw up lines that were not needed, through miles and miles of uninhabited wilderness, merely to insure that another road would not claim the territory first. Inevitably enterprises built on dreams and credit had to collapse; when the dreams failed to materialize, credit also evaporated. The fortunes of other industries, like steel, were bound up with those of the railroads, and when the railroads began to fail one by one in the summer of 1893, the failure quickly spread to other sectors of the economy; thirty-two steel corporations failed during the first six months of 1893. Economic activity in the United States had reached a new stage of interdependence, and a weakness in the very heart of the system unavoidably enfeebled the rest. The same conditions characterized banking. Formerly failures in one part of the country had not necessarily caused failures in other parts. By 1890, however, banking had become centralized in New York, where a large proportion of the country's reserve capital inexorably gravitated. Moreover, these reserves had been freely used in speculation. When stocks fell, many city banks fell with them; and since the city banks held up to 60 percent of the reserves of other banks throughout the country, the panic, once it had seized New York, almost immediately became nationwide.[2]

As members of the humanities, historians have followed the intellectual tradition of describing what they perceive as important cause-effect relationships, hesitating to predict what the future may bring, and hesitating also to prescribe what should be done to prevent destructive cause-effect relationships from repeating themselves. If the historian quoted above had, in retrospect, suggested what should have been done before 1893 to prevent the panic of that year, or what should be done to prevent some future depression, he might have made either of the following suggestions, depending upon his understanding of competitive market systems: Decrying "reckless" and "hasty" decisions that had produced many railroad lines "that were not needed," he might have prescribed improved methods of market research, so that corporate managers with accurate information available to them would not build more rail lines and steel mills than were needed; or, accepting the relationship of the "pressure of competition" to the overexpansion of supply to a point well beyond "any reasonable estimate" of demand, he might have proposed some sort of scheme to restrict, or regulate, the expansion of some or all industries, and also to regulate the use of "reserve capital" for "speculation" (i.e., lending money to many entrepreneurs when a substantial number of them inevitably will be unable to repay their loans).

The historian's analysis is not an unusual one, for many historians have reached similar conclusions about past depressions. If they have fallen short in their analyses, it is only because they have not stripped economic theory and practice to its bare essentials. Had they done so, they would have concluded that it is unregulated competition that, all by itself, causes and sustains an economic depression. The word "regulation" means the placing of limits on production so that all of the output can be sold at or above the costs of production. Put more precisely, this is economic regulation, as opposed to social regulation of health and safety standards. While both will be discussed, I take economic regulation to be the more fundamental requirement, and indispensable if social regulation is to be effective. There is no need to specify at this point how, and by whom, limits on supply should be instituted. Of the two alternative possibilities outlined above, then, only the second makes sense.

Economic slumps are not traceable to —

• greedy capitalist managers who seek short-term profits at the expense of long-term objectives and, in the process, make erroneous estimates of consumer demand for their output;
• inept socialist managers in other countries who, in the absence of enough incentive to achieve efficiency, mismanage their enterprises;
• temporary insufficiency of demand ("underconsumption");
• central bankers (in the case of the United States, the Federal Reserve Board) who are either too tight or too loose with the supply of money;
• policy-makers who are casual about runaway government spending and wasteful programs that only dry up the investment capital needed to produce goods and services for sale; or
• other policy-makers who are callous toward the unemployed, the sick, the needy, and the handicapped, depriving them of even minimal purchasing power in the name of necessary "belt-tightening."

This list includes all or most of the complaints most widely voiced in this regard, and all of them are incorrect. To repeat, unregulated competition stands alone as the cause of an economic slump, a panic, recession, or depression; and this chapter seeks to explain why this must always occur when a freely competitive market is left to its own devices. Stripped to fundamental essentials, the most desired economic transaction involving any good or service can be visualized as a decision-making process that begins with the formation of a temporary organization comprising one buyer (of any good or service) and many sellers (of the same good or service). On paper, the organization looks like this:

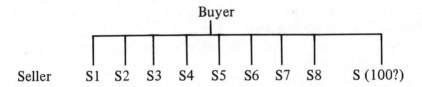

The purpose of competition is to make the individual consumer a "boss" who demands that sellers provide her with many alternatives from which to choose each good or service she desires. Using the analogy of Paul Samuelson, the Keynesian Nobel laureate, the consumer exercises "sovereignty" by "voting" for one seller while rejecting the others. The Nobel monetarist, Milton Friedman, insists that unless each buyer is "free to choose," there can be no competitive market in shirts, shoes, or steel. On this most fundamental matter, economists and other commentators of all economic persuasions differ not at all. A Ralph Nader study group, for example, approvingly borrows the 80-year-old declaration of the U.S. Supreme Court:

> Many sellers compete for the consumer's dollar, and consumers, in turn, buy the best products at the lowest prices. By "voting" with his dollars, the consumer determines the types, quantities, and prices of goods to be produced. The result is that economic resources are allocated among users to maximize consumer satisfaction. Sellers who want to survive the competitive struggle must constantly increase their efficiency and seek out product innovations. "The unrestrained interaction of competitive forces," summarized the Supreme Court as early as 1904, "will yield the best allocation of our economic resources, the lowest prices, the highest quality, and the greatest material progress."[3]

Unfortunately, the "lowest prices" are well below the costs of production in a highly competitive market, for there is no law or mechanism to ensure that prices will not collapse. As I shall emphasize later, the need to cut costs in order to lower prices has the effect of lowering quality, not raising it. To the extent that there is "material progress" at all, it occurs only in fits and starts, heavily punctuated by busts that give the lie to the economists' insistence that a free market always tends toward an equilibrium position. Finally, the notion that an "unrestrained" competitive market yields "the best allocation of our economic resources" is such an obvious absurdity that it is amazing that anyone still attempts to insist otherwise. How can a theory be so wide of the mark? It simply ignores the most basic aspects of the phenomenon with which it deals, in this case the buyer-seller relationship itself.

When each of a number of sellers offers the consumer a good or service when only one of them can make a sale to that consumer, the latter maximizes efficiency by rejecting all sellers except the one providing, from the perspective of that consumer, the best buy, or the "biggest bang for a buck," so to speak. The greater the number of competing firms in any industry, the greater the number of sellers the consumer must reject at the time of purchase. The rejected sellers must then enter another contest, competing once again for the favor of the next consumer, and the next, and the next, and so on. The market system in any industry consists of the sum total of all of these individual contests. If all consumers are to have available to them the maximum number of alternative sellers from which to choose, and the doctrine of unrestrained interaction of competitive forces is intended to bring this about, the greater must be the duplication of output for all transactions taken together; duplication, or redundancy, of output becomes so excessive that much of the output cannot be sold for the costs of production. The competitive struggle thus plays itself out in an inevitable sequence.

In the attempt to underprice competitors, each producer must offer each customer lower and lower prices if that producer is to get at least some return on the goods and services already produced.*

---

*In principle, the market design assumes homogeneity of output, in which case the buyer makes decisions on the basis of price. In actuality, producers use many forms of non-price competition, for example, quality. Non-price competition, however, does not ameliorate the problems of the market and, indeed,

Firms have little choice but to search for ways to cut costs as much as possible and, because wages and salaries are the most important components of variable costs (those incurred after capital invest-ments), they come quickly to mind. Managers lay off some workers, asking the remaining ones to turn out more goods for the same or lower wages. Ironically, this search for productivity improvement leads to still more output at a time when there already is more output than customers are demanding. The next step is to close down plants where labor costs are high, then move to other parts of the country, or to other countries, where labor is cheaper. Eco-nomic theory and practice have a curious and cruel relationship with management theory and practice, a relationship which tells us much about the science, discipline, or profession of economics.

In principle, the consumer's search for maximum efficiency compels each producer to increase efficiency by using the fewest possible workers while paying them the lowest possible wages. Any production manager's primary functions, therefore, are to increase unemployment and to transform workers into slaves. The funda-mental economic principle is to maximize consumer efficiency by minimizing consumer spending, while the corollary management principle is to maximize producer efficiency by minimizing producer spending. Note that the economic principle has nothing to say about the role of the consumer as a worker, while the management princi-ple ignores the role of the worker as a consumer. Paradoxically, the two approaches join hands in seeking to drive down wages. To the consumer or to the producer, the "ideal" worker cannot afford to buy any of the output he produces. This should not be as surprising as it may appear; free-market theology was invented in the age of slavery and, while slavery has been legally abolished, its principles are as powerful as ever. Meanwhile, the complementary attempts to achieve consumer and managerial efficiency leave no room for any notion of social efficiency. This is left solely to the mythical

---

can act to worsen them. The consumer who opts for higher quality (and higher price) in making one purchase is often unable to buy something else, thereby increasing the excess of supply over demand.

"invisible hand" that ties together all the separate and individual decisions made in the name of consumer or managerial efficiency.*

Economists doubtless would deny that a fundamental premise of the theories they espouse is that workers should be paid slave wages. They certainly would deny that they consciously seek to bring this about, but, if the conscious intention of economists is something that cannot be decided here, the historical record is clear enough. Two items in that record are sufficient to make the point. First, whether one speaks of tenant farmers, coal miners, or factory hands, their wages, working conditions, and living environments have been improved only by government and union intervention in the processes of the free market. Not so many years ago, for example, workers lived in company towns — a condition not all that far removed from slavery. Second, as this is written, a government-mandated minimum wage once again is under attack, on

---

*The most fundamental principle of management, applicable in both public and private organizations, is efficiency, defined as the highest possible ratio of output to input when $E = O/I$. All attempts to increase productivity are linked to this principle, but the social anomaly is overlooked. In observing the principle, each manager seeks to employ as few workers as possible when performing any task. Indeed, managers constantly are encouraged to reduce the number of workers (increase unemployment) since this proves the managers are doing their jobs well. Presumably, the savings are distributed to consumers (in lower prices) or citizens (lower taxes). In this context, the worker is not viewed as a citizen. The social objective of providing gainful employment (at decent wages) for as many members of the labor force as possible is wholly outside the boundaries of economic theory and principles.

Concluding a four-month investigation at a time of high unemployment, the Wall Street Journal observed that conditions in "labor camps" in Louisiana resemble those of early 19th-century "slave camps" for those laboring on sugar plantations. Workers are lured by newspaper advertisements promising high wages on off-shore drilling rigs. Camp operators demand powers of attorney, then cash all checks. Kept locked in rooms except when taken to work, the "employees" are charged outrageous prices for food and lodging (plus 50% interest each week for small loans, and $150 for "transportation" to work sites). Owned by prominent citizens, the camps often are labeled "drug and alcohol abuse centers." Superintendents routinely have long prison records for such crimes as grand larceny and murder, but just as routinely are designated as deputy sheriffs. Workers who leave often find they have nothing, and still owe money to the camps. See Wall Street Journal, June 22, 23, 1983. All this is wholly in accordance with basic economic principles that are independent of ideology. The herding of dissidents into forced labor camps is only another method of increasing managerial efficiency by making slaves of workers.

grounds that it acts to keep unemployment at unacceptably high levels — the idea being that jobs would be plentiful if wages were substantially reduced. Left to its own devices, a free market acts to depress wages more and more, not because entrepreneurs are innately greedy and exploitative, but because a free market compels them to do this.

The silent premise of economic theory is that each consumer is a person of independent means, one whose demands for goods and services are givens. The question of how the consumer arrived at a position enabling her to state those demands is not a part of the basic theory of the free market. In making each decision to choose one seller while rejecting all others, however, each consumer uses one of the most fundamental principles of management, a principle too easily forgotten: that because duplication is inefficient and wasteful, it should be eliminated and that, as the manager of her realm, the consumer does so by rejecting all but one seller. The fundamental principle of economics, of course, is that competition is efficient, so that economic principles and management principles are somewhat at odds with each other. Or are they?

The economic sequence begins with a consumer's demand, then proceeds with many producers responding to that demand. As each consumer makes a decision to buy from one seller while rejecting all others, each consumer presumably maximizes her efficiency by allocating her resources so as to achieve the greatest benefit for herself. The logic of economics is that, as every individual consumer realizes the best possible set of outcomes for herself, the overall allocation of resources is, by definition, efficient. When all consumers have made their individual decisions, mountains of goods and services must unfortunately remain unsold, and those who produced them must remain uncompensated for having done so. Economic theory recognizes this to some extent by emphasizing the risks in starting up a business, but the theory then ignores the socially unacceptable outcome by wishing it away. A single example will suffice.

In principle, the failure of any business indicates that the inefficient operator has been forced out by more efficient competitors, so that any bankruptcy is a signal that the market for a particular good or service is working well. Using this logic, central to economics, free-market systems are working better in the 1980s than at any time since the Great Depression of the 1930s. With more bankruptcies than at any time since then, we should rejoice at such a demonstration of market efficiency. This, of course, is nonsense. Firms fail because the basic function of a market is to ensure that much more is produced than can be sold, and there is no reason to assume that only the most inefficient firms fail.

The conclusion is inescapable. Economic and managerial principles are addressed to somewhat different definitions of efficiency (consumer vs. producer), so they cannot be said to directly contradict each other. What can be said, however, is that if society as a whole is perceived to be a social organization, then the economic sequence that leads to maximizing the efficiency of each individual consumer leads also to gross inefficiency for society as a whole. Put simply, a free market destroys society in the attempt to help individual citizens satisfy their individual desires.

The analysis of economic theory and practice hardly can end here, but the foregoing outline includes the essentials. The outline remains valid even if the theory is reversed so as to provide that producers actually create consumer demand, rather than responding to it. One version of this concept holds that large firms "manipulate" consumer demand through advertising and the peer pressure it generates to "keep up with the Joneses," while contemporary supply-side economics argues that if, through new investment and product innovation, more output is produced, consumers will somehow be found for it. Whether creating or responding to demand, the basic requirement is for many sellers to seek out the same potential customer, thereby ensuring that much will not be sold.

If the overbuilding of railroads and steel mills, along with over-expansion in other industries and in credit, caused the depression of 1893, this was not the result of either greed or faulty management, but the outcome of having a free market function precisely as it was supposed to function. Managers then and now are not to be condemned for their failure to follow sound economic and management principles, but are to be extended our sympathy for doing precisely that. Unrecognized and unacknowledged though it may be, the purpose of a free market is to have it collapse into chaos. In the sequence outlined above, the ultimate outcome is inevitable; mountains of goods and services will be left unsold. As I shall indicate, the pattern varies only a little. While agricultural surpluses do indeed climb to unbelievable heights, manufacturers merely shut down and release workers when they know they cannot sell their output. Economists plying their trade, like political scientists plying theirs, have spent their time studying the trivial aspects of their field, not the fundamentals. Perhaps a look at the deeper wellsprings of economic thought will serve not only to reinforce this outline of the inevitable economic sequence, but to show how the modern world fell prey to a wholly unsupportable theory.

THE ORIGINS AND INTELLECTUAL FRAUD
OF FREE-MARKET THOUGHT

Adam Smith's *The Wealth of Nations* appeared in 1776, soon enough to make his work significant to people in this country. While some still view Smith as the founding father of everything bad associated with laissez-faire capitalism, his principal target was centralized authority. As one who "voiced a swelling antagonism to hierarchy and bureaucracy,"[4] he is best described as a "liberal reformer" dedicated to reducing the power of the mercantilist monopolies of his time.[5] As the handmaiden of Western individualism, his free-market theory was extraordinarily attractive then, and remains so today. The issue to resolve, however, is: Precisely what new form of social action was adduced by free-market thinkers as the appropriate substitute for the hierarchies of the eighteenth century? On this matter, economic thinking vacillates quite a bit.

A staunch defender of free markets, Friedrich A. Hayek, has expressed the essence of individualism. The "growth of commerce," he has argued, has been closely associated with the curbing of "despotic political power" and with the enhancement of the individual man's ability to make "his own views and tastes . . . supreme in his own sphere."[6] Yet many other defenders of free markets, especially those who attack government intervention of any sort, praise markets for doing a "remarkable job of coordinating the activities of countless numbers of people who have no idea that they are cooperating with each other and benefiting other people by the actions that they take to benefit *themselves*" (emphasis in original).[7] Such phrases as "mutual cooperation" and "voluntary exchange" appear regularly as guiding principles of economics, to such an extent that two questions must be put to rest.

The first question is whether a philosophy of individualism is an attack upon the concept of authority, and the answer is "no."

Suppose, for example, that any individual (A) makes a decision; if the decision is to have social meaning, it must affect at least one other individual (B). If B must accept A's decision in order to preserve A's right, as an individual, to make that decision, then B must obey A, regardless of what B might prefer to do. In this sequence, A's right to make a decision effectively removes B's right to decide. If, on the other hand, A and B were required to reach a mutual agreement, with neither having coerced the other, the agreement could only be described as a collective one. Individualism, therefore, is nothing more than a disguised restatement of authoritarianism, except for the unlikely example of the hermit whose decisions have no social meaning.

The corollary question is whether economic thought and practice reflect individualism or, rather, the ethic of collectivism reflected in such phrases as "mutual cooperation" and "voluntary exchange." The dominant concept of "consumer sovereignty" expresses the standard economic view that a competitive market cannot exist unless each consumer has many (or at least several) sellers from which to choose. The word "demand," which connotes consumer dominance over the decision process, clearly implies that the consumer should be in a position to coerce sellers into offering the lowest possible price. In principle, that price is offered under duress, and thus the offer cannot be wholly voluntary. This is obscured by the economic convention of focusing upon the final agreement to buy and sell, rather than upon the entire sequence that includes one buyer and many sellers. In principle, free-market theory is an inverted version of a hierarchy, in that it attempts to remove the authority of a monopoly producer to control output, fix prices, and maximize profits; and then to give each consumer authority over the many producers at her beck and call. "Consumer sovereignty," not "voluntary exchange," is the individualistic, not the mutualistic, basis of economic thought.

In his contemporary critique of economic thinking, Lester Thurow demonstrates, perhaps unintentionally, just how powerful is the underlying premise of "consumer sovereignty." He bemoans what he sees as an undesirable combination. The labor market, which accounts for 85 percent of domestic income, is by far the largest of all markets, and determines the "center of gravity" of the entire economy; but the discipline of economics ignores labor-market behavior by compartmentalizing the study of labor economics into what are often entirely separate university departments. The rest of the profession, he concludes, does not have to think about labor at all. Along with his conservative counterparts, unfortunately, Thurow accepts the theory of "voluntary exchange," but if "consumer sovereignty" is the basic theme — and I suggest it must be — the disregard of labor economics becomes wholly understandable.[7] Consumers, not workers, are the focus of economics, and labor economics is a minor activity outside the mainstream, but this is only part of a larger pattern.

As a discipline, science, or profession, economics has used a number of devices over the years to obscure — perhaps intentionally, perhaps not — the implications of free-market theory. Whether they recognize it or not, economists have a vested interest in overlooking evidence that free markets are wasteful, inefficient, and unstable by definition. This might account, at least in part, for the decision to emphasize the final agreement of buyer and seller. Once that decision is made, it becomes easier to invent other devices that obscure the inherent chaos of free markets.

Nothing is more common, for example, than to read about the relationship of supply and demand, and the "law" which governs the relationship. This has the effect of masking the more fundamental relationships among one buyer and many sellers. It is an easy move from this device to the discussion of aggregate supply and aggregate demand, an analytical approach that treats supply and demand as if they could be brought into balance, or equilibrium. This led early in the nineteenth century to Say's Law (1803): the statement that any market system will generate enough demand to buy its own output. Yet aggregate supply must always greatly exceed aggregate demand if each consumer is to make choices from many alternatives. Too easily ignored is a more correct definition of "aggregate" supply, i.e., the sum total of responses that all competing suppliers make to all demands of all consumers. The only possible result is large-scale redundancy. This is not to imply that if, say, 100 steel companies offer each prospective buyer the ton of steel he seeks, the total output of steel, or the total plant capacity for making it, will be precisely 100 times the magnitude of the demand for steel. It is sufficient to repeat that output, capacity, or both, must, by definition, greatly exceed demand.*

---

*Say's Law was preposterous from the beginning, but even its supposed critics accept it. As to the law, it is obvious that a single auto plant can turn out many more cars than can be used by the original resource owners from

Yet another device is to suggest that, as producers become more and more efficient at reducing costs, and that, as they lower prices, elasticities of demand will take hold; new buyers, who might not previously have been able to afford a good or service, will step forward to buy all that is produced. This device not only ignores the basic relationship of one buyer to many sellers, but also overlooks the consequence of constantly declining costs. All too often, wage reduction is the method for reducing costs, but this has the effect of reducing purchasing power as well. Demand elasticity, then, does not take into account the roles of workers as consumers; as a concept, it cancels itself out. In principle, lower prices will increase demand, but economists forget that lower wages must decrease demand somewhere.

The deepest foundation for economic thought, however, may lie in the widely held belief that every human being has material wants that are infinite and insatiable. This assumption, central to the philosophy of the modern West, if not to that of the entire world, leads economists to conclude that because those wants never can be fully satisfied, the overproduction of goods and services is logically impossible. The conclusion is reinforced by the obvious fact that many people are ill-fed, ill-housed, and ill-clothed, so that output does not yet meet all the needs of all the people in the world. On this matter, economists are guilty of imprecise thinking at best.

The concept of infinite demand cannot withstand close scrutiny. As economist Robert Mundell puts it:

---

whom the plant's operators buy what they need to make the cars. The law avoided this problem by using the fallacious double-bookkeeping of economics, which I take up in Chapter 6; it is simply assumed that anything produced can be sold for the costs of production. Keynesianism disputed the law only to the extent of arguing that government intervention is sometimes needed to increase demand to the level of supply, thereby making the law come true. Contemporary supply-side economists are true believers in the law, arguing that taxes, for example, should be cut so as to stimulate the additional supply that is needed; this assumes that taxes are an unwise intervention that prevents the law from operating. Disputes, therefore, concern only the best method to use in carrying out the law. There is no disagreement on the fundamental principle that supply and demand should be in balance, the impossible dream of free-market economics.

If a man had all the money he could possibly use, his activity would be conditioned by scarcity. He would still have to allocate his time if only because life is limited. In choosing a meal, a man has to take account of the fact that his stomach is limited even if he is rich enough to ignore the expense of buying the meal.[9]

Indeed, many economists seem thoroughly confused about the fundamental claim that economics is the "science of allocating scarce resources." Given the individualistic basis of the field, "scarcity" pertains only to the situation facing the individual, not to either society or the world as a whole.* As Mundell notes, this definition has nothing to do with whether the individual is rich or poor. If every individual were infinitely rich, economic scarcity would remain, and freely competitive markets would still turn out much more than could be sold.

In addition, many economists who argue that production should be stepped up, so as to meet the needs of human beings, often fail to notice that if needs are one thing, demands are something else again. The marketplace brings together buyers and sellers, and those who are not prepared to buy do not constitute the demanders. Indeed, those without the wherewithal to buy are not viable members of the market and, in principle, do not exist. Indeed, it is contradictory for free marketers to argue that many human beings have basic needs that are unmet, while simultaneously arguing that government should not subsidize such people so that they can buy what they need.

The corollary premise of economics, hardly ever articulated with precision, is that there are essentially no physical limits to the availability of natural resources. This is the implicit assumption of antitrust laws that encourage the maximum possible number of producers to enter any industry, in the belief that no matter how many do so, the resources are available to support them. While the debate of the last decade over limits to growth is only tangential to the purposes of this book, it can be noted that because free-market theory depends upon the assumption that there are infinitely available natural resources (or infinitely possible substitution),

---

*Leaders of public and private organizations, including governments, do indeed allocate organizational resources but, in principle, the resources were obtained from individuals.

any acknowledgment that resources are finite must be accompanied by an admission that freely competitive markets cannot function in such conditions.

While the science of economics has strayed far afield from its beginnings, important aspects of those origins remain with us. Many universities offer degrees in applied economics, consumer science, or home economics (though that title has been abandoned by many universities because of the connotation that it represented only a second-rate degree granted young women training for a career in managing the households of their affluent husbands). Economists were only too eager to turn their attention to advising presidents instead of housewives, because they, too, disliked facing the origins of their field. Yet in a section of the newspaper entitled "Home," a *Washington Post* feature story of January 20, 1983, was labeled "The Dilemma of Deciding: Do You Want a Decorator?" The front page carried the photograph of an apparently affluent wife, perhaps 40 years old. Sitting in her "office," surrounded by estimates from decorators that were fastened to a corkboard wall, and closely examining swatches of material (presumably for carpeting, drapes, or furniture), she pondered the choice of some offers over others. As an "applied economist" doing comparison shopping for the family, just as Nancy Reagan carefully studied alternative proposals for replacing the White House china, this homemaker was carrying out the fundamental purpose of economics.

This, and this alone, is economics, whatever economists might prefer to believe. Two major variants of applied economics are simply inversions of the basic design. First, when a firm or a public agency uses economic concepts in managing its affairs, applied economics takes on the label of "management science." Were it not for minimum-wage laws, managers would do comparison shopping for workers willing to accept slave wages, because the managers would have no other choice. Management science, therefore, is only the science of creating unemployment and starvation. The second variant is used when government seeks to contract with private business for the provision of public services, or studies alternative solutions to public problems. Under such headings as "competitive bidding" and "policy analysis," government does comparison shopping for the best solution at the lowest cost. Without the interventions of laws that require government itself to pay prevailing wages — laws often assailed because they allegedly cause "unjustified tax increases" — government itself also would seek to pay slave wages (it does not now enforce laws providing that government contractors must pay prevailing wages).

While no practicing economist is intentionally callous or cruel, the science compels those using it to demonstrate such characteristics. As one example, take the situation of each individual consumer vis-à-vis every other consumer, a relationship acted out almost every day. The interest of each consumer is to have slave wages paid to every worker who produces goods or services the consumer may buy. Widespread depression among farmers is often cited in the headlines as follows: "Declining Food Prices Benefit Consumers." In an industrial area near Pittsburgh (Steel Valley), one of the most bitter teachers' strikes in local history recently concluded. The blue-collar-union families in the area resolutely opposed teacher demands for salary increases, acting out the behavior patterns induced by our market theories. Each consumer seeks the best wage or salary for herself, but opposes high wages for others. A poll in that area would have shown that steelworkers believed teachers were overpaid, and vice versa.

As a second example take the situation of workers in an industry long known as the originator of the sweatshop. The International Ladies Garment Workers' Union recently noted that apparel imports had increased from 3.6 percent of all garments sold in the U.S. in 1957 to 41 percent in 1982. Imports from China rose 47 percent in 1982, as the U.S. government sought to find markets in China for other American products. The average Chinese garment worker was being paid 16 cents per hour; the average American, $4.94. The union, estimating that 660,000 more Americans would have jobs if no garments were imported, asked the government to reduce imports to 25 percent. A spokesperson for the American Retail Federation thereupon declared that "the wider the access to a market, the better for the consumer."[10] Countless such examples demonstrate the schizophrenia of economics, which deals separately with consumers and workers, showing little concern for the latter.

The most cruel aspect of economics, however, is its sweeping under the rug of the problem of unemployment. The two major factors of production are labor and capital, and labor costs are best held low by ensuring that a pool of unemployed workers is always available and can compete with those at work by offering to accept lower wages. If the overproduction of goods and services is needed to keep prices low, an oversupply of labor is needed to keep wages low. Political debates about acceptable and unacceptable levels of unemployment mask the requirement, of any market economy, to have some minimum level of unemployment at all times. Even in the best of times, full employment is an impossible objective. The irony is that while economists insist that overproduction is basically impossible, they accept an oversupply of labor as both necessary and desirable.

One scholar concludes that "unemployment has become a permanent feature in most industrialized countries."[11] The U.S. Employment Act of 1946, which assigned government a responsibility for the health of the economy, was not named the Full Employment Act for just that reason. The point is that not only are people jobless because it is a social duty for some to be jobless (they are not guilty of anything), but governments everywhere routinely permit unemployment to rise, in the hope that this will stop inflation. In this context, policies encouraging unemployment perform the same function as antitrust laws; i.e., the purpose of oversupply (labor) and overproduction (goods and services) is to hold down prices for the ultimate benefit of the sovereign consumer. Unfortunately, the result is low-paid or unemployed workers who no longer are consumers.

NOTES

1. Engels is excerpted in Robert V. Daniels (ed.), *Marxism and Communism: Essential Readings* (New York: Random House, 1965), p. 10; Marx's view is in his "Wage-Labor and Capital," in *Selected Writings*, Vol. 1, p. 82, quoted in Bertell Ollman, *Alienation: Marx's Conception of Man in Capitalist Society* (Cambridge: At the University Press, 1971), p. 180; the contemporary Marxist view is E. K. Hunt and Howard J. Sherman, *Economics: An Introduction to Traditional and Radical Views* (New York: Harper & Row, 1972), p. 33.

2. Harold U. Faulkner, *Politics, Reform and Expansion: 1890-1900* (New York: Harper & Brothers, 1959), p. 145.

3. Mark J. Green, ed., *The Closed Enterprise System: Ralph Nader's Study Group Report on Antitrust Enforcement* (New York: Grossman, 1972), pp. 5-6.

4. Charles E. Lindblom, *Politics and Markets: The World's Political-Economic Systems* (New York: Basic Books, 1977), p. 33.

5. Eli Ginzberg, *The House of Adam Smith* (New York: Octagon Books, 1964), foreword.

6. Friedrich A. Hayek, *The Road To Serfdom* (Chicago: University of Chicago Press, 1944), p. 14.

7. Alan C. Stockman, "Paul A. Samuelson's ECONOMICS, Eleventh Edition," in Craig Bolton et al., eds., *American Economics Texts: A Free Market Critique* (Reston, Va.: Young America's Foundation, 1982), chap. 1.

8. Thurow, op. cit., pp. 215, 222.

9. Robert A. Mundell, *Man and Economics* (New York: McGraw-Hill, 1968), p. 7.

10. *USA Today*, May 10, 1983.

11. David Macarov, *Work and Welfare: The Unholy Alliance* (Beverly Hills: Sage, 1980), p. 90.

2

Economics in Peace, War, and Recent History

I have been unable to discover an economist who has argued that free-market competition must inevitably lead to overcapacity, overproduction, and a steep depression. I have located two, however, who have concluded that, under certain circumstances, overproduction can require intervention. In this sense, both are Keynesians, in that they imply or assert that overproduction is better defined as temporary "underconsumption"; i.e., the solution is to stimulate demand. Their arguments — one of recent vintage, and one made long ago — make the larger point that in conditions of overproduction, producers have little choice but to ask for government help. Such interventions have taken two forms that are mirror images of each other. I shall label them "interventions to prevent collapse" and "expansion by imperialism and war."

When the inevitable overproduction occurs, the obvious need within any one society is to limit further overproduction so that prices and wages will not collapse. The necessary interventions can range from paying producers to stop producing (a form of unemployment compensation widely used in agriculture), to having government buy the surplus (also in agriculture), to erecting trade barriers that prevent foreigners from entering home markets. Such solutions can be labeled those of "protectionism," "isolation" or even "autarky." Conversely, an overproducing industry deliberately may seek to capture foreign markets, and the history of imperialism may be traceable to such attempts. If the first approach (limit supply) begins with the assumption that demand is stable (inelastic), and cannot quickly be increased, the second solution (increase demand) assumes that new customers can quickly be found, even if they must first be conquered by military force. Both approaches transcend ideology, being traceable to the organization of market systems, not to the political beliefs of participants.

A third form of government intervention, or regulation, has occurred only once in modern history, even though the intervention never has been acknowledged in the way I propose herein. Whatever the intentions of those who fought World War II, the consequences were those of economic regulation. This was the first war in which much of the world's existing industrial capacity was leveled by aerial bombing. The effect was to restrict competition by destroying the most important competitors. Since the United States was the only large industrial country to emerge unscathed, its prosperity was assured for the next two decades — i.e., until Europe and Japan reindustrialized, and until developing countries built some industries of their own.

A second aspect of World War II economic regulation was less unique in effect, but equally unrecognized. American prosperity during the war was not traceable to a Keynesian remedy (stimulation of demand through full employment), but rather to the regulation of the home-front supply. The existing industrial overcapacity in the United States was put to work producing military hardware (the "arsenal of democracy"). Consumers, many enjoying higher living standards than ever before, even were subjected to the rationing of many important commodities. In making these somewhat novel arguments, I do not seek to trivialize history; quite the contrary. The economists are the trivializers; they routinely ignore the impact of such cataclysmic events as war. Because they do not understand that competition causes depressions, they cannot understand how and why the United States recovered from the Great Depression. Marxists trivialize by blaming capitalism when that is not the problem at all. My purpose, then, is to show how, in theory and practice, economic regulation becomes fundamental to prosperity and stability.

As I shall indicate, I am not wholly in agreement with the analyses of the economists from whom I borrow, for, as economists, they were trained to reject the theory offered herein. In both cases, they fail to see the inevitable and destructive waste of freely competitive markets. Significantly, however, their analyses are based much more upon an organizational, social, or collective perspective than is normal among economists.

INTERVENTIONS TO PREVENT COLLAPSE:
A "COMMON" INTEREST

In dissecting what must happen in a perfectly competitive market, Mancur Olson used the concept of a "common," or "group," interest that, in principle, is foreign to the basic theory of economics. As I shall point out, his use of the concept accounts in part for what I take to be the flaw in Olson's analysis, but his words are worth our attention:

> The firms in a perfectly competitive industry . . . have a common interest in a higher price for the industry's product. Since a uniform price must prevail in such a market, a firm cannot expect a higher price for itself unless all of the other firms in the industry also have this higher price. But a firm in a competitive market also has an interest in selling as much as it can, until the cost of producing another unit exceeds the price of that unit. In this there is no common interest; each firm's interest is directly opposed to that of every other firm, for the more other firms sell, the lower the price and income for any given firm. In short, while all firms have a common interest in a higher price, they have antagonistic interests where output is concerned. This can be illustrated with a simple supply-and-demand model. For the sake of a simple argument, assume that a perfectly competitive industry is momentarily in a disequilibrium position, with price exceeding marginal cost for all firms at their present output. Suppose, too, that all of the adjustments will be made by the firms already in the industry rather than by new entrants, and that the industry is on an inelastic portion of its demand curve. Since the industry demand curve is by assumption inelastic, the total revenue of the industry will decline. Apparently each firm finds that with price exceeding marginal cost, it pays to increase its output, but the result is that each firm gets a smaller profit. Some economists in an earlier day may have questioned this result, but the fact that profit-maximizing firms in a perfectly competitive industry can act contrary to their interests as a group is now widely understood and accepted. A group of profit-maximizing firms can act to reduce their aggregate profits because in perfect competition each firm is, by definition, so small that it can ignore the effect of its output

on price. Each firm finds it to its advantage to increase output to the point where marginal cost equals price and to ignore the effects of its extra output on the position of the industry. It is true that the net result is that all firms are worse off, but this does not mean that every firm has not maximized its profits. If a firm, foreseeing the fall in price resulting from the increase in industry output, were to restrict its own output, it would lose more than ever, for its price would fall quite as much in any case and it would have a smaller output as well. A firm in a perfectly competitive market gets only a small part of the benefit (or a small share of the industry's extra revenue) resulting from a reduction in that firm's output.

For these reasons it is now generally understood that if the firms in an industry are maximizing profits, the profits for the industry as a whole will be less than they might otherwise be. And almost everyone would agree that this theoretical conclusion fits the fact for markets characterized by pure competition. The important point is that this is true because, though all the firms have a common interest in a higher price for the industry's product, it is in the interest of each firm that the other firms pay the cost in terms of the necessary reduction in output needed to obtain a higher price.

About the only thing that keeps prices from falling, in accordance with the process just described, in perfectly competitive markets is outside intervention. Government price supports, tariffs, cartel agreements, and the like may keep the firms in a competitive market from acting contrary to their interests. Such aid or intervention is quite common.[1]

One flaw in this argument is basic to economic theory. In principle, there can be no group interest that is known to, or understood by, members of the group, in this case the producers of any given good or service. The theory of the "Invisible Hand" is that while society's interest will be served by the workings of the free market, no member of that market (buyer or seller) will have in mind anything at all except his own individual interest:

Every individual endeavors to employ his capital so that its produce may be of greatest value. He generally neither intends to promote the public interest, nor knows how much he is promoting it. He intends only his own security, only his own gain. And he is in this led by an Invisible Hand to promote an end which was no part of his intentions. By pursuing his own interest he frequently promotes that of society more effectively than when he really intends to promote it.[2]

It follows immediately that no member of a group who makes decisions on the basis of his individual interest can possibly act in ways that are contrary to group interests, because, in principle, group interests are automatically served by decisions based wholly on one's individual interest.

The logic becomes clearer, I think, when a second flaw is outlined. In making his argument, Olson used the example of any perfectly competitive industry that "is on an inelastic portion of its demand curve"; i.e., no matter how much prices may fall, additional consumers cannot be found. Olson's implicit assumption seems to be that if demand were sufficiently elastic, buyers would pay reasonable prices for all the output. Olson, that is to say, accepted the conventional economic doctrine of demand elasticity, concluding that, except in very unusual situations, it is not necessary for producers to seek government intervention. The argument implies that Keynesian economics is valid, in that insufficient demand, not excess supply, is the problem. Yet it is the limitless duplication of competition that remains the problem.

If Olson accurately described in 1965 why intervention (regulation) is often necessary, he has argued more recently that interest groups, or lobbies, separately formed by producers and workers for the purpose of bringing about intervention, are the fundamental causes of stagflation and "social rigidities." In elaborating further upon his earlier logic, he concludes, in effect, that because the "cure" (intervention) is worse than the "disease" (collapsing prices), all forms of regulation should be abandoned so as to establish an environment conducive to accelerated economic growth. He implies, that is to say, that even though conditions of inelastic demand may cause whole societies to collapse, intervention is sinful. Having strayed ever so slightly from the economics fold, Olson has returned home.[3]

Leaving aside Olson's slightly flawed logic, his original argument shows why members of many industries have so often found it necessary to ask for interventions that have the effect of protecting them from the inevitable ravages of perfect competition. Because people in this country (and in other countries as well) have been taught that free markets do indeed work well, an industry seeking help (as the steel and auto industries do now) is immediately labeled as trying to substitute political action for economic efficiency. Labor and management are thought greedy, and uninterested in improving productivity. These reactions are not only traceable to long-term socialization, but also to the situation in which, as noted earlier, every consumer's interest is to have every other worker, and every firm except the one in which the consumer works, subject to intensive competition so that the consumer will pay the lowest possible price.

The interventions Olson lists (price supports, tariffs, and cartel agreements) are only a few of the many that have been used, and interventions will loom large in the examples I use in this book. The purposes of the interventions are to prevent prices from falling below costs of production, restrict the number of alternatives available to consumers, or even enable producers jointly to plan the total output of all firms in an industry. Along with other interventions, they regulate supply — a form of intervention that is adopted with great reluctance, industry by industry, because each regulatory intervention is seen as an exception to the norm of unrestricted competition. Our policy structure has for years been a crazy quilt of such interventions, each a supposedly temporary adjustment required only because of unusual conditions. The strength of economic theology masks the reality that economic regulation is the norm, and that unrestricted competition is the undesirable exception.

A depression would not occur if supply were consistently and adequately regulated, so the fact that we have had many depressions indicates that our malady is one of to little regulation, not too much. The results of uninhibited competition, however, seldom have been confined within the boundaries of any one society. I turn now to the work of the late British economist, J. A. Hobson, to suggest that the roots of imperialism and war are to be found in freely competitive markets.

EXPANSION BY IMPERIALISM AND WAR

J. A. Hobson's analysis of the origins of imperialism was published in 1902, but at least some of the language is familiar to the readers of today's newspapers:

> The spirit of adventure, the American "mission of Civilization," were, as forces making for Imperialism, clearly subordinate to the driving force of the economic factor. The dramatic character of the change

is due to the unprecedented rapidity of the industrial revolution in the United States from the eighties onwards. During that period the United States, with her unrivalled natural resources, her immense resources of skilled and unskilled labour, and her genius for invention and organization, developed the best equipped and most productive manufacturing economy the world has yet seen. Fostered by rigid protective tariffs, her metal, textile, tool, clothing, furniture, and other manufactures shot up in a single generation from infancy to full maturity, and, having passed through a period of intense competition, attained, under the able control of great trust-makers, a power of production greater than has been attained in the most advanced industrial countries of Europe.

The history of any of the numerous trusts or combinations in the United States sets out the facts with complete distinctness. In the free competition of manufactures preceding combination the chronic condition is one of "overproduction," in the sense that all the mills or factories can only be kept at work by cutting prices down towards a point where the weaker competitors are forced to close down, because they cannot sell their goods at a price which covers the true cost of production. The first result of the successful formation of a trust or combine is to close down the worse equipped or worse placed mills, and supply the entire market from the better equipped and better placed ones. This course may or may not be attended by a rise of price and some restriction of consumption: in some cases trusts take most of their profits by raising prices, in other cases by reducing the costs of production through employing only the best mills and stopping the waste of competition. . . .

We are not here concerned with any theoretic question as to the possibility of producing by modern machine methods more goods than can find a market. It is sufficient to point out that the manufacturing power of a country like the United States would grow so fast as to exceed the demands of the home market. No one acquainted with trade will deny a fact which all American economists assert, that this is the condition which the United States reached at the end of the century, so far as the more developed industries are concerned.

Industrial and financial princes in oil, steel, sugar, railroads, banking, etc., were faced with the dilemma of either spending more than they knew how to spend, or forcing markets outside the home area. Two economic courses were open to them, both leading towards an abandonment of the political isolation of the past and the adoption of imperialist methods in the future. Instead of shutting down inferior mills and rigidly restricting output to correspond with profitable sales in the home markets, they might employ their full productive power, applying their savings to increase their business capital, and, while still regulating output and prices for the home market, may "hustle" for foreign markets, dumping down their surplus goods at prices which would not be possible save for the profitable nature of their home market. So likewise they might employ their savings in seeking investments outside their country, first repaying the capital borrowed from Great Britain and other countries for the early development of their railroads, mines and manufactures, and afterwards becoming themselves a creditor class to foreign countries. . . .

Overproduction in the sense of an excessive manufacturing plant, and surplus capital which could not find sound investments within the country, also forced Great Britain, Germany, Holland, France to place larger and larger portions of their economic resources outside the area of their present political domain, and then stimulate a policy of political expansion so as to take in the new areas. The economic sources of this movement are laid bare by periodic trade-depressions due to an inability of producers to find adequate and profitable markets for what they can produce.

The process, we may be told, is inevitable, and so it seems upon a superficial inspection. Everywhere appear excessive powers of production, excessive capital in search of investment. It is admitted by all business men that the growth of the powers of production in their country exceeds the growth in consumption, that more goods can be produced than can be sold at a profit, and that more capital exists than can find remunerative investment.

It is this economic condition of affairs that forms the taproot of Imperialism. If the consuming public in this country raised its standard of consumption to keep pace with every rise of productive powers, there could be no excess of goods or capital clamorous to use Imperialism in order to find markets: foreign trade would indeed exist, but there would be no difficulty in exchanging a small surplus of our manufactures for the food and raw material we annually absorbed, and all the savings that we made could find employment, if we chose, in home industries.

The prime object of the trust or other combine is to remedy this waste and loss by substituting regulation of output for reckless overproduction. In achieving this it actually narrows or even dams up the old channels of investment, limiting the overflow stream to the exact amount required to maintain the normal current of output. But this rigid limitation of trade, though required for the separate economy of each trust, does not suit the trust-maker, who is driven to compensate for strictly regulated industry at home by cutting new foreign channels as outlets for his productive power and his excessive savings. Thus we reach the conclusion that Imperialism is the endeavour of the great controllers of industry to broaden the channel for the flow of their surplus wealth by seeking foreign markets and foreign investments to take off the goods and capital they cannot sell or use at home.[4]

Obviously, "dumping" surpluses abroad was as familiar to Hobson as it is to those today who attack Europeans and the Japanese for selling in the United States for less than production costs. Our government, however, recently prepared to sell surplus cheese abroad on the same basis — because government warehouses bulge with the output of the dairy industry. While Hobson's analysis is worth bringing up-to-date, particularly with respect to implications not included in the passage quoted above, he relied too much upon Say's Law (i.e., that any market can generate enough demand to buy its output). As Keynes argued later, Hobson believed that redistribution of wealth would give lower classes the purchasing power to absorb everything produced in England. If, in his view, imperialism was unnecessary, he overlooked the logic of competitive duplication. Even so, it was unusual for an economist to ask for wage increases, as Hobson did during the Great Depression:

> To many business men and to some economists it will seem preposterous to propose high wages . . . as a [remedy] for unemployment. . . . To raise wage-rates in a business which can barely meet costs is seen to be impractical. And so it is if the policy is tested by application to a single business, or even a single trade. For this separatist application does not provide the expansion of demand which alone can validate the policy. . . . To raise wages in the motor industry . . . would not cause workers in this trade to buy many more motors. . . . But if . . . the high wage policy were simultaneously applied to all or most occupations, the general increase in consuming power . . . might easily provide a sufficient new fund to meet the higher wage bill out of the reduction in overhead costs due to the full continuous use of plant, etc.[5]

Hobson's analysis fell short by underestimating the importance of regulating supply, although some agree even now that it can be necessary to protect infant industries by guaranteeing them local markets until they are viable, even if they cannot remain viable if regulation is withdrawn. The engines of production turn out much more than can be sold and, even though many lived in poverty (one-fourth of the English at the turn of the century) when Hobson wrote, producers enlisted government help in finding foreign markets. With industrial states all doing the same thing, and with enough wealth to support large armies, military forces expanded everywhere.

The Marxist-Leninist view, conversely, was that domestic producers sought only to export capital, not goods, because "backward" areas were sources of cheap labor.[6] Since Hobson allowed for this, he agreed with part of the Marxist view, but both analyses missed the larger point: It was, and is, an environment of competition that compels producers, on the one hand, to duplicate each other's investments, thereby ensuring overcapacity and overproduction, and, on the other hand, to seek the cheapest possible labor at home or abroad. These disastrous outcomes are traceable to the good intentions of economic competitors (seeking to serve consumers), not to their allegedly bad intentions (seeking to exploit workers). The patterns remain unchanged, but ideologues persistently misdefine the problem. Capitalists and socialists alike are innocent victims, not the reciprocal targets, of conscious evil.

Hobson wrote in a somewhat cautious manner. Rather than attacking capitalists for unremitting greed, he implied sadly that producers were trapped. Those forming trusts and combines had to seek some form of regulation, even if they did not realize that global competition must become increasingly unstable. And he dismissed the nineteenth-century argument, still a staple for some economists, that "want of confidence" contributes to a depression, an argument made in his time by J. S. Mill and A. C. Pigou:

> Here we have the explicit explanation of a purely objective phenomenon, an excess of unsaleable articles by reference to what is properly and primarily a purely subjective phenomenon, want of confidence. Want of commercial confidence can no more be a cause of an accumulation of unsaleable goods than a rise in the thermometer can be a cause of sunshine. . . . Want of confidence . . . is nothing but a subjective interpretation of the already existing fact of a general excess of forms of capital, or productive power. It may be a convenient term to describe the attitude of mind of those who have money to invest and who refuse to place it, but it can furnish no explanation of the congested state of industry implied by the fact of general oversupply.[7]

Today, the lack-of-confidence argument amounts to saying that if only producers can be made to feel more optimistic, they will build more steel mills in a world already having too many.* When the dominant theology holds that no matter how much is on hand, more always is needed, it is small wonder that theologians resort to such foolishness.

Hobson's approach can be translated into the everyday jargon of modern managers. Among large firms, competition for market shares is the norm, each manager seeking to maintain or improve his position. If there are, say, four large firms in an industry, each accounting for 25 percent of the sales, each manager may seek to increase his share to 30 percent. By analogy, the customers of each firm become "natives" to be conquered through "invasion of the territory." This is a zero-sum game, since any firm's increase in market share must be accompanied by a decrease in the share(s) of one or more other firms. In principle, each firm's workers are only "soldiers" to be supported at minimum wages. Global competition among large firms, then, always threatens to become a conflict among states themselves.

The analyses of Olson and Hobson indicate that, as historians have concluded, overproduction recurs again and again in market systems. The two economists, however, are incorrect in implying that the problem can be solved by stimulating demand. The problem is not ameliorated at all by shifts in demand elasticity. If this assertion is correct, then much of the history of the past half-century should be more understandable.

THE GREAT DEPRESSION

Unemployment in the United States generally is estimated to have reached 25 percent in the 1930s; today, unemployment fluctuates, by season and area, between 9 and 15 percent, with some regions at higher levels. A condition in which 75-to-90 percent of the labor force is at work cannot accurately be labeled a "collapse." Free markets, then, can lead to widespread poverty, social unrest, and even political revolution, but a total collapse is unlikely. Something akin to a total collapse, however, can occur in modern war,

---

*One must keep in mind the schizophrenia of economics. When investor confidence is sought, the emphasis is upon less consumption and more savings. When consumer confidence is the objective, the emphasis is reversed.

and I suggest that when some societies collapsed in World War II, the consequences were similar to those of economic regulation. In this discussion the Great Depression must first be understood.

If overproduction is the cause of depressions, not merely an effect mislabeled as "underconsumption," then the primary indicators of trouble are agricultural surpluses and, to a lesser extent, industrial inventories accompanied by idle capacity. Because the agricultural sector has long approximated a "perfect" market of innumerable producers, it has most often been afflicted with overproduction. Indeed, one economic historian concluded years ago that the ceaseless (not temporary) "trials and tribulations" of American farmers over a 60-year period could be summarized in the single proposition that *"the supply of farm products as a whole has exceeded the demand for them at prices which cover the costs of most farm units."*[8] So it was in the 1920s, remembered as a decade dominated by prosperity.

U.S. agricultural output was stable through the decade, maintaining a level about 15 percent higher than in 1919-21, but new competitors in the grain markets (Canada and Argentina) caused stagnation here.[9] With the onset of the depression, farm prices dropped by 1932 to less than half the already-low prices of 1929. In a classic example of the sequence described by Olson, total farm output in 1931 actually increased by $1 billion over 1930, because "millions of small, individual farmers reacted to falling prices by working harder to try to maintain their receipts."[10] The more they tried, of course, the worse things became, surpluses piling up all around.

Industrial activity began turning downward in 1929, in a "familiar inventory recession."[11] Even with demand estimated correctly, the many producers responding to the demand turn out more than can be sold, then curtail their own buying — and price-wage spirals begin. For those who now worry about inflation, wholesale prices dropped by 16 percent in 1931; in Germany by 13 percent; in the Netherlands by 20 percent; in Great Britain by 18 percent; and in Japan by 21 percent.[12] Inventories do not accumulate in the same manner as farm surpluses do when times are bad. When sales decline, plants shut down or operate at inefficiently lower levels. The situation was made worse because wages in the 1920s had not kept pace with increases in productivity, a fact well known to those in today's labor movement who face complaints that wage increases recently have exceeded productivity gains. One careful estimate is that productivity in the 1920s rose two to three times as fast as real wages (purchasing power).[13] Stock market fluctuations are more dramatic than these indicators, but the latter are more significant.*

MOVING TOWARD REGULATION

It is startling now to realize that during the last years of the Hoover administration and the early years of the Roosevelt administration, there was considerable agreement about the causes of the Great Depression and about some of the cures for it. This has been obscured by what happened later, in both the everyday world of political maneuver and the mythical world of economic theory. The *New York Times* editorially praised bituminous-coal operators for suggesting in 1931 that the industry be regulated; it might make sense, said the editorialist, to treat the industry as a public utility, so that the recognized problem of overproduction could be solved; only the antitrust laws obstructed sensible solutions.[14] A few months later, however, the Department of Justice warned that antitrust action would be taken if operators put into effect the regional sales agreements they were developing. Yet it was widely recognized that the coal being sold could be produced by only half the coal miners then available.[15]

In his annual message for 1931, Hoover suggested amending the antitrust laws because "destructive competition" had led to "great wastes" and "demoralization" in such industries as coal, oil, and lumber.[16] Senator David I. Walsh of Massachusetts introduced legislation early in 1932 to authorize a "curtailment of production" under certain circumstances.[17] Almost a year later, Hoover's attorney general sought temporary revisions in the antitrust laws to solve the overproduction problem.[18] Railroad executives

---

*When wages lag behind productivity, the effect is one of forcing workers to save, the savings being transferred to management. The contemporary equivalent, now under consideration, is a consumption tax to be levied not upon what people earn, but on what they spend; since only the affluent can save much of what they earn, the regressive effects are obvious. As was the case in the 1920s, the underlying assumption is that more capital is always needed for yet more investment in new plants. Typically, consumption taxes are advocated by liberals and conservatives alike.

met throughout 1932 in efforts to "avoid preventable and competitive waste."[19] Both Hoover (in 1931) and Roosevelt (in the 1932 campaign) advocated removal of "duplication and waste" in railroad service, as well as regulation of the expanding trucking industry that, competing with railroads, had created chaos in the national transportation system; William Z. Ripley of Harvard echoed the dominant view: that competition must be restrained.[20] The *Times* praised Roosevelt's plan for the railroads as statesmanlike and thoughtful.[21]

Early in 1933, the president of the American Banking Association argued for amending the antitrust laws to permit "intelligent control of output,"[22] and, a few months later, Roosevelt outlined the economic theories of the New Deal. In a fireside chat in May, he promised to do something about "disastrous overproduction" in agriculture, and to "encourage each industry to prevent overproduction," "We have found our factories able to turn out more goods than we could possibly consume," he asserted, adding that "antitrust laws were not intended to encourage unfair competition that results in long hours and starvation wages and overproduction." Roosevelt's target was "cutthroat competition."[23]

The aim of the New Deal was to reduce productivity, a cardinal sin to economic theologians. In 1982 a television program, commemorating the hundredth anniversary of Roosevelt's birth, featured an old newsreel clip of Roosevelt explaining his theory: "If we can only persuade employers to keep wages up while reducing working hours, we can put people back to work." This was anything but a Keynesian prescription for a recovery, as Keynes himself noted in 1934. As he put it, "I have no belief in the efficacy [for direct stimulus to production] of the price- and wage-raising activities" of the New Deal.[24] While Keynes favored a "pump-priming" (a government injection of money into the economy), he had no use for economic regulation. What was entailed in FDR's program, so often mislabeled Keynesianism?

The centerpieces of the New Deal were the National Industrial Recovery Act (NIRA) and the Agricultural Adjustment Act (AAA). The former authorized cartels and price fixing, as well as efforts to spread work and keep up wages, while the latter made it possible to restrain farm output. The Blue Eagle became the national symbol for any industry whose firms developed a "code of fair practice" (557 codes by 1935) to raise wages, shorten working hours, and keep prices up.[25] Making good on the many recommendations to amend antitrust laws, the NIRA actually suspended them. Unfortunately, theology reasserted itself before long. Reaffirming the traditional commitment to antitrust laws, free competition, and periodic depressions, the Supreme Court destroyed the NIRA in 1935 on grounds that Congress had illegally delegated its powers to the president. In contemporary jargon, the Supreme Court "deregulated" the economy. National income had risen from a low of $40 billion in 1933 to $57 billion in 1935 but, following the NIRA's demise, the old sequence returned. Deregulated output quickly jumped but, by 1937, inventories once again were piled high.[26] A second crash occurred in 1937-38, and only World War II brought a recovery.

Not only were economists not disposed to rush to the defense of the New Deal, but, by 1935, Herbert Hoover was thinking about running for office again. Reversing his 1933 support of the NIRA,[27] he weighed in with a ringing indictment:

> This whole idea of ruling business through code authorities with delegated powers of law is un-American in principle. . . . These codes are retarding recovery. They are a cloak for conspiracy against the public interest. The whole NIRA scheme has saddled the American people with the worst era of monopolies we have ever experienced. However monopoly is defined, its objective is to fix prices or to limit production or to stifle competition; . . . [this is] Fascist regimentation.[28]

The agreement on solutions for the Great Depression never was complete, of course, especially with a Democratic president regulating industry, and more especially when scattered indicators of recovery appeared in 1933 and thereafter. Alfred P. Sloan of General Motors, for example, resolutely opposed the New Deal and, by drastically pruning output and workers, managed to keep his firm profitable. By September, 1935, Sloan was attacking the proposed Social Security Act, asserting that "we certainly are not going to tolerate any further interference with recovery [now that] the depression is definitely behind us."[29] This was about two years before the automobile industry experienced truly substantial labor problems as the United Auto Workers struggled for legitimacy. In the case of GM in the 1930s or, say, Chrysler in the 1980s, it is relatively easy to retain or restore profitability by laying off large numbers of workers and imposing wage cuts on those remaining.

Hoover's 1935 attack is reflected today in the words of one analyst who would blanch if labeled a disciple of Hoover: Judge Stephen Breyer, once a staff assistant to Senator Edward Kennedy, when the latter led the drive for deregulating the airlines and trucking, recently looked back on the Roosevelt years:

The framers of the National Industrial Recovery Act . . . believed that agreements among firms not to cut prices would increase profits, encourage investment, and maintain purchasing power. Thus, ordinary competition in many industries was viewed as "excessive." The NIRA cure for recession, however, has been discredited. In a world in which competition is the desired norm and regulation the exception, the NIRA theory does not provide a coherent rationale for selective regulation.[30]

Breyer's view is the dominant one today, but it is a misreading of history. The New Deal was anything but "selective." It was an attempt to regulate all industries because duplicative overproduction was seen as having reached epidemic proportions. If that history is largely forgotten now, it is because so much attention has been given to Keynesian economics. Essentially, Keynes held the standard view: that overproduction was impossible,* even if Say's Law might occasionally need help in the form of demand stimulation.

I do not wish to imply that the New Deal program was perfectly coordinated, but it was logically consistent. Roosevelt not only sought to cure the disease of overproduction by reducing each worker's output, but to reduce the labor force as well. Those newly entitled to social security pensions were put on notice that they would lose benefits if they worked very much. Such provisions seem discriminatory now, in that a low-income retiree cannot work while one with investment income is not penalized. Yet the purpose was to keep over-65 workers out of the labor force while enabling them to live in decency. Laws against child labor had the same effect. Taken as a whole, the program sought to reduce output,

---

*To be precise, economists admit (as in Olson's analysis) that overproduction, or an excess of supply over demand, can occasionally occur. In general, however, they conclude that this is only a "temporary imperfection," and that any attempt to "cure" it by intervening in free-market processes can only create other problems that are even worse.

share work, and sustain purchasing power. Only the latter was Keynesian.

The New Deal, gutted by mid-1935, never had much of a chance. Its theoretical flaw lay in the belief that economic depressions were temporary anomalies requiring only temporary remedies. Those implementing the policies, therefore, were alert to the slightest signal that a recovery had begun, for this would justify a return to normalcy. When the Supreme Court intervened, Roosevelt's program became wholly Keynesian by default, even if true Keynesians thought the program should have applied more stimulus than it did. From my perspective, of course, Keynesian demand stimulation cannot produce a recovery by itself; so the six remaining years before World War II saw little in the way of a recovery.

REGULATION IN WORLD WAR II

It is well to remember that even in 1941, a year which ended with the Pearl Harbor attack, unemployment in the United States averaged 10 percent (5.5 million). A year later, joblessness had dropped to 1.5 million, and for two wartime years, unemployment never exceeded 1 million.[31] These figures are worth remembering also, for they indicate that when jobs are available, unemployment can be kept at about the 2-percent level. The war initiated a long period of prosperity, but the reasons for that prosperity never have been acknowledged because they lie outside the boundaries of economic theory.

The war furnished a reason for putting idle workers and plant capacity to use, even if much of the output was, by economic definition, "wasteful" military production. The armed forces (and American allies) provided so much demand that home-front rationing became widespread (involving gasoline, tires, fuel oil, sugar, coffee, meat, and canned and packaged goods). Prosperity depended upon regulation of supply. In the absence of these restraints, prosperity would have been impossible. To put it in reverse, full employment could not have brought prosperity by itself. Meanwhile, the war had the long-term effect, which has yet to be understood, of regulating global competition by destroying much of the world's industrial capacity. Overcapacity, after all, can be eliminated in many ways and, even if those who did the bombing did not have this consciously in mind, regulation was the consequence. This was the only war in which this has occurred, and those who analyze economic matters hardly ever take such things into account. It became inevitable that the United States would experience a long period of prosperity until European and Japanese reindustrialization (and the building industries in developing countries) would again lead to a glut of industrial capacity.

This is not to imply that capitalism requires war for the sake of sustaining itself. As one observer noted, exactly the same prosperity could have been produced by "crisscrossing the country with superhighways and building hospitals, schools, and underground urban parking facilities."[32] As I shall later argue, this observation is valid today; if production for sale is to be held within the limits of demand by restricting competitive duplication, large-scale public-works programs make sense, especially when more of them are always needed. Any claim that Keynesian economics — only a minor variant of the conventional theology — brought prosperity to the United States or any other country is as nonsensical now as it has always been.

In looking back at the unlearned lessons of the Great Depression and the war, one factor deserves special emphasis now, as the prelude to a more extended analysis later in this book. Politicians and economists of all persuasions have constantly worried more about government deficits incurred to build public works and military hardware than about private deficits incurred to build plant capacity. The competitive duplication of a free market, unfortunately, makes it more likely that much of the industrial-plant capacity will not be needed, while the items built by government are likely to be needed. Even when government-produced items turn out to be unneeded, as in the case of much of the military output in World War II, throwing them away turns out to be more beneficial to the economy than either seeking buyers for them or turning to industrial production instead.

Combining Theory and History

Imperialism, if Hobson was correct, is attributable to the search for markets, even if customers must be conquered first; this makes some military action a form of coercive advertising. By analogy, global free trade always has been a form of imperialism, even when obscured by economic jargon. When leaders proclaim today that America must meet the "competitive challenge," they mean that the United States should take customers away from the producers of other countries. Ironically, such recommendations always imply that other countries have succeeded where the United States has failed, yet it is clear that other industrial countries have about the same problems.[33] In retrospect, the initial attempt to recover from the Great Depression was not only peaceful, but noncompetitive. It appears that Italy, Germany, and Japan sought to follow the historical pattern of military expansion, and, indeed, the latter's search for a "Greater East Asia Coprosperity Sphere" ultimately led to a collision with this country.

One need not be a Marxist determinist to point out that if free-market competition leads only to a severe depression, then there is a great propensity for producers to ask their governments for assistance in serving those who demand and need the production, including those living in other countries. Supposedly peaceful competition, that is to say, becomes a first step toward war, the likely outcome when economic and political factors come together. In this sense, expenditures on public works could become an alternative to military production. Tragically, the manufacture of bombs is more easily accommodated by political theory than is the building of bridges by economic theory.

As innumerable political candidates proclaim, however, there is a persistent yearning for peace and prosperity. It follows that if unregulated free markets lead only to depressions, there must be considerable evidence that the original New Deal was only a more extreme example of an equally persistent effort to avoid a depression by regulating supply. Whatever the textbooks say, and whatever candidates say as well, regulation must be more a norm than an exception. Once this idea is grasped, the evidence is easily located. I turn now to an examination of the many forms economic regulation has taken.

NOTES

1. Mancur Olson, *The Logic of Collective Action: Public Goods and the Theory of Groups* (New York: Schocken, 1969), pp. 9-10.

2. Quoted in Craig Bolton et al., eds., *American Economics Texts* (Reston, Va.: Young America's Foundation, 1982), p. 17.

3. Mancur Olson, *The Rise and Decline of Nations* (New Haven and London: Yale University Press, 1982), esp. chaps. 1, 2, 7.

4. J. A. Hobson, *Imperialism: A Study*, 3d ed. (London: George Allen & Unwin, 1938), pp. 74-85.

5. J. A. Hobson, *Poverty in Plenty* (London: George Allen & Unwin, 1931), p. 65.

6. On the Marxist-Leninist views of Hobson, see E. K. Hunt and Howard J. Sherman, *Economics: An Introduction to Traditional and Radical Views* (New York: Harper & Row, 1972), p. 128.

7. J. A. Hobson, *The Problem of the Unemployed* (London: Methuen, 1896), pp. 121-22, quoted in John Allett, *New Liberalism: The Political Economy of J. A. Hobson* (Toronto: University of Toronto Press, 1981), p. 22.

8. Ross M. Robertson, *History of the American Economy* (New York: Harcourt, Brace, 1955), p. 390.

9. Murray R. Benedict, *Farm Policies of the United States, 1790-1950* (New York: Twentieth Century Fund, 1953), p. 277.

10. Harry N. Schreiber, Harold G. Vatter, Harold Underwood Faulkner, *American Economic History* (New York: Harper & Row, 1976), p. 358.

11. John Kenneth Galbraith, *The Great Crash*, 3d ed. (Boston: Houghton Mifflin, 1972), pp. 179-80.

12. Goronwy Rees, *The Great Slump: Capitalism in Crisis, 1929-1933* (New York: Harper & Row, 1970), pp. 85-86.

13. Robertson, op. cit., p. 558.

14. *New York Times*, August 8, 1931, p. 12.

15. Ibid., February 6, 1932, p. 3; February 7, 1932, p. 14; and April 3, 1932, sec. 9, p. 3.

16. Ibid., December 9, 1931, p. 21.

17. Ibid., January 25, 1932, p. 5.

18. Ibid., August 17, 1932, p. 25; December 18, 1932, sec. 3, p. 5.

19. Ibid., December 8, 1932, p. 13.

20. Ibid., December 9, 1931, p. 21; June 22, 1932, p. 37; and September 18, 1932, sec. 1, p. 3.

21. Ibid., September 19, 1932, p. 16.

22. Ibid., January 17, 1933, p. 4.

23. Ibid., May 8, 1933, pp. 1-2.

24. Reprinted in ibid., April 10, 1983, sec. 3, p. 2.

25. Robertson, op. cit., p. 562.

26. Kenneth D. Roose, *The Economics of Recession and Revival: An Interpretation of 1937-1938* (New Haven: Yale University Press, 1954), p. 183.

27. *New York Times*, October 1, 1933, p. 29.

28. Herbert Hoover, "The NRA," in his *Addresses Upon the American Road, 1933-1938* (New York: Charles Scribner's, 1938), pp. 45-57.

29. Ed Cray, *Chrome Colossus: General Motors and Its Times* (New York: McGraw-Hill, 1980), p. 282.

30. Stephen Breyer, *Regulation and its Reform* (Cambridge: Harvard University Press, 1982), p. 30.

31. Robertson, op. cit., p. 565.

32. Ibid., p. 566.

33. *America's Competitive Challenge*, A Report to the President of the United States from the Business-Higher Education Forum (Washington, D.C., April 1983). The American "decline" and "stagnation" are measured in terms of the success of other countries in "capturing" major market shares in many industries. Presumably, "economic malaise" is curable only through a "recapture"; see pp. 2-3.

3

The Wide, Wide World of Regulation

If free markets cannot sustain themselves, it follows that economic regulation, even if not specifically labeled as such, is necessary for the continued viability of any industry. I suggest in this chapter that regulation can take many forms, and that the examples to follow do not, by any means, give a complete picture. Systems of economic regulation become easier to discover, however, once it is accepted that every industry must have one if stability is to be achieved. The popular image of a public regulatory body that supervises the operation and prices of an electric-power company is misleading, in that many different regulatory schemes can act to dampen the effects of all-out competition by stabilizing output and prices. As in farming, an obvious solution is to reduce production or buy it at fixed prices. In the hidden form of regulation that stabilized American manufacturing industries for so long a time, competition was dampened out of fear that the winners would become monopolies subject to prosecution.

To many readers, one of the arguments in this chapter will appear novel, and perhaps wholly inappropriate. If World War II provided the impetus for U.S. prosperity by bombing away the competition, prosperity was sustained by an unacknowledged form of economic regulation that neither the regulators nor the regulated industries themselves fully understood. If a corporate executive fears that his competitors will capture an increasing share of the market for his product, he also fears that if his firm is too successful, the U.S. Department of Justice may undertake antitrust action against it. For some of the large firms, especially in the 1950s and 1960s, decision-making was analogous to tightrope walking. When Robert S. McNamara was president of the Ford Motor Company, his firm would buy each year one of the first Chevrolets produced, take it to a special room, and then dissect it piece by piece to discover how General Motors had been able to save perhaps a tenth of a cent on a particular item.[1] Yet executives also believed that upon occasion, they should compete less vigorously for an increased market share than would have been the case if antitrust intervention were not a possibility. Such interventions usually follow from ex post facto decisions, in that nobody can know in advance precisely what data will entice the antitrust enforcers to act. In working out a theoretical argument, hypothetical examples are often needed. The reader will have to decide, for example, if General Motors could have sold more autos than it actually sold during its best years.

In this chapter, I look at the two principal types of markets in which economic regulation has been the norm, not the exception. Even if some industries are generally believed to be highly competitive, persistent economic regulation of them is often overlooked. No case is more historically persistent than agriculture.

REGULATION IN HIGHLY COMPETITIVE MARKETS

Because agriculture has long been the industry most closely resembling the mythical free market, it has perennially suffered from overproduction and economic hardship. Because governments for many years refused to accept a responsibility to regulate prices and output to some extent, farmers tried many times to regulate themselves through marketing cooperatives. The original concept of the farm cooperative, both in the United States and Canada, was to have farmers hold their crops off the market until prices rose enough to cover production costs. Not only was this extraordinarily difficult to accomplish (when some members break ranks, a cooperative quickly disintegrates), but, if farm cooperatives had become completely successful in organizing on a regional or national scale, they would have become the equivalent of monopolies. In principle, cooperatives might have been subject to accusations that they were causing people to suffer by refusing to sell them food.

Yet numerous attempts were made in the 1920s to set up large-scale cooperatives, and even to socialize all the associated industries important to farmers. The Nonpartisan League, for example, suggested that state-owned mills, elevators, and banks be established within producer states, and that government take over the ownership and operation of the transportation and communications systems critical to farmers. The league was prominent for a time in Minnesota and North Dakota, retaining control of most offices in the latter state for many years. Collectives in cities and on farms became less and less popular after the Soviet Revolution, however, so it was left for the Great Depression to demonstrate that government would have to massively intervene if the country's food supplies were not to be threatened.[2]

If the period from the Great Depression until the present is taken as a whole, regulation has taken so many forms that it is virtually impossible to list them all. The tragedy is that many of these interventions have been disguised so as to give the appearance that government is not regulating agriculture when, in fact, it is. A representative list of what government has done, and is doing, might include at least the following:

• all sorts of refinancing arrangements, including loans guaranteed by government, to enable farmers to retain farms threatened by foreclosures;

• acreage allotments, i.e., government planning as to how many acres should be devoted to certain crops, followed by allocations to the states and, ultimately, to individual farms;

• making advance loans to farmers on the basis of projected output and prices; if prices fall, the government takes the crop, but if prices rise, farmers sell the crops, pay off the loans, and keep the difference; the loans, with interest, become minimum prices guaranteed by government;

• direct government purchases of surplus crops pegged at parity prices, i.e., prices having the same purchasing power as in favorable earlier years;

• marketing agreements — i.e., with government approval, producer associations set minimum prices, plan the total quantity to be produced, then allocate it among producers (occasionally, viewers see television films of mountains of excess oranges left to rot so as to reduce the number brought to market);

• food-stamp and other nutrition programs (school lunches) that help the poor, but that gain their initial impetus from the need to dispose of farm surpluses while keeping up market prices;

• subsidizing exports through bounties, i.e., paying exporters the difference between the "artificially high" prices at which they must buy within the country and the lower world prices at which they sell — i.e., dumping;

• all sorts of tariffs and quotas to protect American agriculture from inroads in the domestic market by foreign suppliers;

• the use of surplus crops as an instrument of foreign policy, sometimes in the form of aid to other countries; if the altruistic outcomes are sometimes emphasized, the need to stabilize agriculture remains the basic motivation.

Responding to the problem of bulging government warehouses, President Reagan in 1983 launched a program known as Payment in Kind (PIK), or, as he described it, a "crop swap." In return for agreeing not to plant new crops, farmers would be given crops already in storage and permitted to sell them.[3] This, in effect, is unemployment compensation, and only another form of regulation that restricts output as a way of supporting prices. As in the Great Depression, however, farmers taking the year off could not be expected to buy farm machinery and other supplies at the normal rate.*

Like other examples to be mentioned, farming has some unique aspects. The output in any given year is heavily dependent upon unpredictable weather (1983 is an excellent example) and, for some products (cattle, hogs), two to four years can elapse between the time a decision is made to increase output and the time products are ready for market. These natural interventions and time lags

---

*As the year wore on, it was clear that the overall cost of price-support programs would remain high, ranging from $21 billion to $37.5 billion, with only $22 billion projected for net farm income, now constantly declining because of global overproduction. The secretary of agriculture suggested a "market-oriented" approach tied to free-market prices (*New York Times*, May 20, 1983). Because he assumed that price supports caused overproduction, and that free-market prices would be above production costs (both assumptions were incorrect), he was heading toward a farm collapse. A public-works approach to agriculture logically would involve direct payments to farmers for taking steps to slow down soil erosion.

make it difficult to prove beyond question that regulation is either needed or can be effective. The initial agricultural programs of the Roosevelt years, for example, coincided with the dust-bowl years, so that an observer can conclude that the droughts of 1934 had more to do with decreasing output than did New Deal regulation. It is more important to note that the bad weather generally helped the agricultural sector by acting to hold prices up.[4] Once the sequence of free competition and overproduction is understood, agriculture's uniqueness becomes less significant than its similarity to other industries.

The prevailing opinion is that all these government interventions, except perhaps for some of those during the darkest years of the Great Depression, are motivated solely by political considerations. The use of the word "political" connotes attempts by some groups, in this case farmers, to gain an unfair advantage over other groups. When King Cotton reigned, congressmen from cotton-producing areas were routinely accused of helping their constituents at the expense of the broader public interest. Richard Nixon and John Connally were portrayed as helping the dairy industry in return for campaign donations and votes, and Senator Jesse Helms now stands condemned for helping tobacco farmers.

To economists who work most closely with theories of economic regulation, this is an academically respectable view. The most prominent among them is George Stigler of the University of Chicago, a recent Nobel winner. He summarizes his view as follows:

> We propose the general hypothesis: every industry or occupation that has enough political power to utilize the state will seek to control entry [into the industry or occupation] . . . by new rivals; . . . an industry seeks higher profits by obtaining public control of entry. . . .[5]

Stigler pays less attention to agriculture than to such industries as transportation, but the farm vote clearly is important to politicians seeking it, and government policies to restrict farm output and keep prices up are not intended to encourage new entrants into agriculture.

Similarly, political analysts sometimes attack laws and regulations that permit the affected farmers to participate in the decision process that provides them with economic support.[6] Commodity groups, for example, are allowed to vote on supports; yet allowing large numbers of farmers to cast ballots on support proposals is not much different from government-sanctioned collective-bargaining decisions. Policy-makers and analysts have yet to face the obvious need for systematized and permanent forms of regulation. It is not enough to merely argue that farmers should be turned loose to take their individual chances in selling what they grow.

The argument and evidence outlined above indicate that the long-term problem of farmers (and other industries, such as textiles) has been overproduction, defined as more output than can be sold for the costs of producing it. To the farmers, the theoretical equilibrium of the free market, which keeps supply and demand in balance, and provides reasonable profits, has been nonexistent. Yet Stigler's basic premise is that industries seek regulation to gain higher profits, when the public interest is that they be content with the normal profits they can expect in an unfettered market. If economic regulation is needed, therefore, output controls for the sake of keeping prices up must logically be accompanied by the discouragement or prevention of new entrants into the regulated industry. If economic regulation is needed in all industries, then some limit on new entry into them is a well-nigh universal requirement.

The question of new entry will be more directly related to some of the examples that follow than it is to farming but, in principle, the new-entry question arises in all industries. I have been troubled for some time with this aspect of the meaning of economic regulation, but there is no way to escape the compelling logic: Economic regulation ultimately must require some attention to both entry and exit. Competitive duplication inevitably leads to having too many firms in all industries, and any solution must prevent still more firms from making things even worse than they already are, while making sure that other firms leave the industry.

As in many other industries, the question has not been faced in agriculture, but there are reasons for avoiding it. As mentioned above, farm output is inherently unpredictable, and the worst possible outcome would be a food crisis brought on by having too little available for survival of the population. In common with individuals in other industries, moreover, many farmers have seen no reason to pack up and leave, because jobs for all unneeded farmers might not be readily available elsewhere. On balance, then, the policy of supporting farmers has been wholly defensible, even if it has led to the piling up of enormous surpluses. Americans are mistaken, by the same token, in pointing to the enormous productivity of the agricultural sector. While overproduction may be a necessary and even desirable form of inefficiency, there is no reason to label it efficiency.

The dominant interpretation must be dismissed out of hand as related only to myth, not reality. Farmers have sought political solutions because the free market provides no solution at all. They have sought help because they had to, and they have found themselves the victims of runaway policy schizophrenia. Grain deals with the Soviet Union have become indispensable to the farm economy, but foreign policy is whipsawed. Jimmy Carter embargoed shipments in retaliation for the Soviet move into Afghanistan, but even hardliner Ronald Reagan lifted the ban after making a campaign promise to do so. The Soviets can be punished only by damaging farmers as well, and this makes little sense.* And, when government seeks to economize by cutting back on nutrition programs, it punishes both the poor and the farmers.

The tragedy is that economic theology has conditioned most Americans to believe that government regulation of agriculture, too little though it may be, results only in "artificially high" prices for those shopping at supermarkets. The phrase "artificially high" can have no meaning at all, however, except through an implicit comparison with "natural free-market" prices and, if the latter are only depression prices, then "artificial" prices are needed everywhere. Poignant examples abound.

A front-page article in the *New York Times* of November 27, 1982, was accompanied by a picture of a Long Island potato farmer

---

*By the summer of 1983, the Payment-in-Kind program had taken on a slightly different shape. Farmers had agreed to keep so much land idle that the government was running short of surplus stocks of wheat with which farmers would be compensated for ungrown wheat. Surplus stocks were low because the government had committed 44 million bushels of wheat to a cut-rate flour sale to Egypt. In subsidizing a huge sale (dumping), the government was fighting a trade war with European countries by underpricing them. This, in turn, was forcing the government to encourage farmers to grow wheat solely for the purpose of returning it to them to meet PIK agreements. The subsidies for growing wheat were estimated to be as high as $20 billion, in a program originally designed to save money. See *Washington Post*, June 16, 1983. Who actually would be punished or rewarded in this case?

who, on his 85 acres, raises potatoes. The farmer, with 42 years' experience, reported that while the current wholesale price for a 100-pound load had fallen from $4 to $3.50, the break-even price was $5.50-to-$6, and that he could not survive if 1983 turned out to be the same. The accompanying article outlined how picking by hand had been replaced during the past decade by mechanization. This had lowered labor costs while increasing production. The headline was as follows: "Despite Big Crop, L. I. Farmers Are Worried." The view that it is always better to produce more and more is so ingrained that it never occurred to the *Times* that a more correct headline would be "Because of Big Crop, L. I. Farmers Are Worried." Such is the extent to which thinking must change.

THE BIG FIRMS: SELF-REGULATION AND ITS DEMISE

The long post-World War II economic boom in this country was not sustained by Keynesian economic policies ("If demand is right, supply will look after itself"[7]), nor by the "Yankee ingenuity" cherished by Americans. Industrial prosperity was sustained by the ability of large firms to regulate themselves in unusual and uncomfortable relationships with large labor unions and, perhaps more important, with the U.S. Department of Justice. In the American pattern of oligopoly, the tendency was for a few very large firms to dominate the market in most industries, usually accounting for more than 70 percent of the sales, industry by industry. In economic jargon, this was, and is, "imperfect competition," in that each of the big firms was strong enough to influence price levels in its industry. Each firm, in what became standard business-school language, engaged in "strategic planning" for its own long-term future, and sought to "control its environment" to whatever extent it could.

The most widely recognized aspect of large-firm decision making was the use of "administered," or "target," prices, often condemned by economists dedicated to the free interplay of market forces, and also by political leaders worried about rising prices in general. John Kennedy became so incensed at one industrywide increase in steel prices (with U.S. Steel acting as price leader) that he used all his presidential clout to compel a temporary rollback. If prices obviously were planned over long periods, congressmen and prosecutors could not prove that the large firms had "conspired" with each other to "fix prices," even though many observers were uneasy about concentrated industrial power. Yet stabilized prices were useful for many reasons.

Prices were set high enough to garner more-or-less guaranteed profits, not only to provide stockholders with reasonable dividends, but also to amass large retained earnings for investment (these accumulations often were triple the size of individual savings).* Stabilized prices enabled producers to enter into long-term contracts with suppliers and with labor. This was important if producers were to plan on anything but a day-at-a-time basis, and just as important to workers borrowing money to buy homes, appliances, and automobiles. Among economists, John Kenneth Galbraith stood almost alone in defending large-scale organizations. He responded as follows to the standard economic criticisms of oligopoly:

> . . . it is the usual claim against the oligopolist that he keeps prices too high and has an undercommitment of capital and labor; it is evident that he makes effective use of capital, organization and technology because he is big and because he is big he is also an oligopolist. No one can ask him to be an oligopolist for the purposes of capital investment, organization and technology and to be small and competitive for the purposes of prices and allocative efficiency. There is a unity in social phenomena which must be respected.[8]

The purpose of this analysis is not to rehash all the old arguments about what is right and wrong in having market power concentrated in a few large firms in most industries. Rather, the purpose is to suggest that the firms not only were large enough to regulate output and prices, thereby preventing the ravages of free-market competition from taking hold, but were virtually compelled to do so. Yes, they were relatively free of foreign competition for quite a few years, and yes, they did compete vigorously against each other

---

*One example indicates how little the concept of "retained earnings" is understood. Regulated power companies generally are prohibited from charging rates high enough to accumulate capital for new plants. They now ask regulatory agencies for permission to levy surcharges upon present consumers in order to finance new plants for other consumers. This has become an important issue in some areas, and the agencies sometimes approve, sometimes disapprove. Yet the practice of raising capital from present customers has been a routine one in private industry.

for market shares. The largest firms in each industry were on notice, however, that if an individual market share became too large, the Department of Justice might initiate antitrust action.

The question to be asked is: If firms such as General Electric or General Motors had competed as vigorously as they could have for larger shares of their markets, could they have increased those market shares? They might at some point have been subject to prosecution for predatory competition (price cutting for the purpose of driving competitors to ruin), or simply for being too big. The United States entered the 1950s and 1960s after the most vigorous period of antitrust enforcement in the history of the Sherman Act, with untold sums having been spent on litigating government efforts at dissolution, divorcement, and divestiture. The government won many of these cases, even if the penalties were relatively mild; in the modern world, large industrial organizations are inevitable. When Judge Learned Hand, among the most renowned of American jurists, decided that the Aluminum Company of America was in violation of antitrust laws by virtue of controlling 90 percent of the market, this reminded corporate managers that bigness alone might subject them to expensive court action, even if all their decisions had otherwise been proper.[9] The Justice Department doubtless was unaware that it actually was restricting competition, because its purpose was precisely the opposite. Yet General Motors, an obvious example, was regularly attacked by congressional committees during the 1950s, when it accounted for half the automobile market. The Supreme Court, ending a nine-year case, decided in 1957 that DuPont must relinquish a 23-percent interest in GM (dating from 1917) because DuPont supplied 50-to-70 percent of GM's fabric, finishes, and anti-freeze. In other antitrust actions, GM was forced in the 1960s to help competing bus manufacturers, and to sell off the plants of its subsidiary, the Euclid Road Machinery Company. Former solicitor general Robert Bork, a critic of antitrust law, describes it as a "subcategory of ideology" that drives the large "antitrust enterprise of lawyers, economists, judges, and legislators." He approvingly quotes Richard Hofstadter's conclusion that "managers of large corporations do their business with one eye constantly cast over their shoulders at the Antitrust Division." Bork concludes that "[if] the law announced a policy of dissolution of any firm that exceeded 50 percent of the market, [any firm approaching that size] would have every incentive to restrict its output in order to avoid the penalties of law."[10] To

Bork, the restriction of competition, not unique to Republican or Democratic administrations, is undesirable; to me, the restriction (which, because of foreign competition, is no longer meaningful) was a desirable, if wholly inadvertent, contribution to prosperity, and the only useful outcome ever achieved by antitrust law. GM executives (and those in some other firms) spent so much time fending off attacks on market dominance that the subject must have influenced marketing and production decisions. Yet the executives could not have been expected to announce that they were acting to restrain competition.

Because no accepted theory completely explains how and why self-regulation worked, many observers remain unaware that it ever existed, do not yet see all its effects, or cannot now understand why it so quickly disappeared. Galbraith's analysis focused upon the ability of large firms to manipulate (regulate) demand by using expensive advertising to persuade consumers to buy. Dan Rather's huge salary, for example, is paid by advertisers who collect taxes from consumers in the form of higher prices. Even though Galbraith's explanation is as complete as any, it ignores the more fundamental regulation of output that was so important to oligopolies.

American industry, its workers, and its consumers generally prospered during the era of self-regulation. Those who preach the virtues of competition often forget that consumers who expect an appliance to last 20 years are better served when companies stay in business that long. Unfortunately, self-regulation is now largely a thing of the past, because American industry no longer stands relatively alone in the world. Beginning with the Marshall Plan, war-ravaged countries rebuilt their industries. Developing countries, with the assistance of international and private banks, borrowed heavily to start up their own industries. American supremacy inevitably gave way to a global economy that is now shaped, for the most part, by free trade and all-out competition across national and ideological boundaries. Self-regulation, that is to say, has been superseded by global overcapacity and overproduction. Even an occasional exception only serves to highlight the pattern. As consumers, Americans yearn for the days when oil-producing countries could not set prices (even if their ability to do so is waning a bit now); but as producers, the same Americans wish there were fewer steel mills in the world. As inventories and excess capacity have come to the fore, international price wars have taken the center stage, and news media are filled with stories of "dumping," "brib-ery," "kickbacks," "false inventories," and even of a notable increase in global industrial espionage.

A depression scenario now unfolds. Many plants are closed or operating well below efficient levels, not because they are "obso-lete," as textbooks would have it, but simply because there are far too many of them in the world. Those adhering to economic princi-ples seek to lower American wages and prices so that our firms can compete with others, but this would only transfer our unemploy-ment elsewhere. The more closely we follow the theories, the more unemployment persists, and the more purchasing power declines or stagnates. Meanwhile, steel operators petition the government for restrictions on imported steel and (shades of the 1930s) ask for the suspension of antitrust laws so that they can move into further consolidations.

Most liberal and conservative analysts would reject this analysis of self-regulation and its demise. Some liberals have long been critics of the ability of large firms to set prices and of the decisions of managers to reduce output, instead of cutting prices. A conserva-tive, conversely, argues that because the prices of large firms have fluctuated along with prices in general, the firms have had much less power than their critics have claimed. Since neither side agrees that overproduction is possible, neither would accept the need for regulation of output. Yet it appears self-evident that General Motors cannot logically be expected to continue producing at near-maximum capacity, taking whatever it can get in a glutted market. Galbraith, who overlooked overproduction, surely was correct in recognizing that large-scale planning was, and is, necessary, and that prices must be "administered."

The disappearing form of self-regulation that carried us through a quarter-century of prosperity may not have been the best system that could have been designed. Market-share competition, for example, is very expensive, as the four gasoline stations on many street corners will attest. It may not be wholly legitimate to raise investment capital through profits, because this makes customers unacknowledged and unrewarded stockholders. Yet there is little doubt that without output regulation, free-market chaos would have engulfed us much earlier. Combined with the effects of World War II and the "hidden hand" of potential antitrust action, self-regulation brought success. With the dominant version of economics,

Keynesianism, emphasizing the management of demand, supply regulation was overlooked, and so now is its demise. Managers did not overlook it, however, and I turn now to examples that indicate the extremes to which those managers will go when they see no other way to accomplish the necessary regulation.

NOTES

1. David Halberstam, *The Best and the Brightest* (New York: Random House, 1969), p. 231.

2. Murray R. Benedict, *Farm Policies of the United States, 1790-1950* (New York: Twentieth Century Fund, 1953), pp. 108, 113, 188.

3. *Washington Post*, January 12, 1983.

4. Benedict, op. cit., p. 312.

5. George J. Stigler, "The Theory of Economic Regulation," in his *The Citizen and the State: Essays on Regulation* (Chicago: University of Chicago Press, 1975), pp. 114-16, 139.

6. Theodore J. Lowi, *The End of Liberalism: Ideology, Policy and the Crisis of Public Authority* (New York: W. W. Norton, 1969), pp. 102-15.

7. Geoffrey Barraclough, "The Keynesian Era in Perspective," in Robert Skidelsky, *The End of the Keynesian Era: Essays on the Disintegration of the Keynesian Political Economy* (New York: Holmes & Meier, 1977), p. 107.

8. John Kenneth Galbraith, *The New Industrial State*, 2d ed. (Boston: Houghton Mifflin, 1971), p. 184.

9. Ross M. Robertson, *History of the American Economy* (New York: Harcourt, Brace, 1955), pp. 497-98.

10. Cray, op. cit., pp. 385-94, 445-47; Robert H. Bork, *The Antitrust Paradox: A Policy at War With Itself* (New York: Basic Books, 1979), pp. 3-4, 197.

4
Regulation by Collusion, or How to Create Criminals

Many seek to turn over to private contractors the delivery of a variety of public services, because they believe that government has "become too large, too expensive, and too intrusive,"[1] and that whenever it is possible to compare private- and public-service provision, the former is found "superior."[2] This is not a new idea. The second Hoover Commission of the mid-1950s adopted, as its central philosophy, the notion that government could benefit by "contracting out," and even Woodrow Wilson's 1887 essay on administration declared that government should "make its business less unbusinesslike."[3] What could be more tempting than to transfer to government the presumed efficiencies of the market?

The current effort to privatize the public sector is one of the most interesting phenomena around, and I suggest it is not coincidental that it coincides with a period of high unemployment. Yet if my argument is correct, attempts to transform the domain of public administration into a free market overlook the fallacies of economic theology. In the Reagan administration, the effort has focused upon user fees; i.e., each citizen should pay, item by item, for the services used. In principle, there are few limits to the concept except, perhaps, for national defense. If normally associated with such concepts as having trucks pay taxes proportional to their use of highways, the principle could easily be expanded:

- An automobile driver might be required to pay for driving on streets, by dropping coins in meters, block by block, since more should be charged for a five-mile trip than for a single block.

• One serious proposal is that a citizen should pay, perhaps by the mile, for Coast Guard help for a boat in distress; and, if enough citizens economize by not calling, the Coast Guard might be abolished.

• Another proposal is to sell all or parts of the country's weather service, and citizens might then pay directly for each forecast they seek.

The theory of consumer choice can be pushed too far, as it is by the advocates of what sometimes is labeled "public-choice" doctrine.

One suggestion is to have federal agencies devise competing program proposals, then have the president and Congress choose from among them.[4] Another would have all levels of government contract out as much as possible, enabling officials to compare public and private performance.[5] Yet another would have local governments "buy" services from each other, police protection being a prominent example.[6] Some seriously believe that citizens should vote directly on every bill before legislatures, punching buttons on television sets or dialing numbers on phones,[7] the results being handed to legislators in the form of computer printouts.* Still other proposals are more widely known; among them are the attempts to amend the Constitution to require balanced federal budgets, referenda to reduce taxes (e.g., California's famous Proposition 13), and the abolition of public agencies unable to periodically justify their existence ("sunset laws"). We are deluged with philosophies that range from advocacy of the "minimal state,"[8] to complete "self-regulation,"[9] to education managed solely by the "consumer sovereignty" of "voucher systems."[10]

Competitive bidding is the oldest and most widely used method of seeking to bring into government the benefits of free-market operations. Indeed, it often is mandatory that public managers use competitive bidding, and they know critics will attack them for using "cost-plus," or "negotiated," contracts. Bidding is attractive because it seems to correspond to the ideal version of the free

---

*This proposal was advanced before the divestiture of AT&T. With local telephone rates now scheduled to rise quickly and steeply, the cost of voting by telephone would become something of a "poll tax." On telephone deregulation, see Chapter 5.

market. When a public agency issues specifications for what it seeks to buy, it insists that every bidder offer precisely identical output. The agency's choice, from among those "fit, willing, able, and responsible," will therefore depend solely upon price. But does this really correspond to free-market theology? If policy-makers and economists believe competitive bidding is pure, then it does not correspond, and those who believe it does are trapped in one of the more monumental confusions that clutter the interface of economic theory and public policy. In principle, a free-market price is identical for all producers at any given moment. If one firm lowers a price (and "price competition" always refers to falling prices, not rising ones), competitors must meet that price (assuming a homogeneous product). The theory assumes a free flow of information, but this is impossible when sealed bids are used to inform the agency awarding a contract. Assuming that all firms are fully qualified, the lowest bidder wins, but those submitting higher bids might be prepared to reduce their prices if given the opportunity. This significant departure from classical theology is often overlooked.

In the everyday world, "we will not be undersold" is a meaningful form of competition. When large firms announce price increases at the same time, however, they are routinely attacked for offering identical prices. Yet if firms bidding on a contract offer identical prices, this is taken as evidence of collusion and, indeed, it may be just that. Ironically, bidders fulfill the basic condition of a free market by offering the same prices. It is possible, then, that collusion and conspiracy lead to precisely the same outcomes as free-market competition, in which case antitrust prosecution is an old breed of cat. Those convicted of collusion or conspiracy are assumed to have cheated, even if the planning had no effect upon ultimate outcomes.[11]

If competitive bidding is so desirable, why does it lead to so many undesirable outcomes? Cost overruns, deliberately understated costs, cheating on specifications, bribery, price fixing, bid rigging, and other forms of illegal planning appear to be reaching epidemic proportions. If, as seems likely, competitive bidding becomes even more widely used than it is now, more and more contractors and public officials will be indicted, convicted, and lodged in already overcrowded prisons. Indeed, competitive bidding has the unintended effect of creating criminals.

Following an analysis of why undesirable outcomes are inevitable, I will turn to four case studies. Three illustrate why contractors find themselves in situations which virtually compel them to violate one law or policy objective in order to conform to other laws and policy objectives. The fourth case is an illustration of how to "get it right," so to speak, but the case demonstrates that desirable outcomes may be possible only when free-market principles are abandoned or substantially altered. My immediate conclusion is that competitive bidding should be abandoned forthwith because it requires excessive competition and duplication among bidding firms. Because the principle cannot be observed, the practice must inevitably be illegal planning, or regulation. Competitive bidding should be replaced by consensual, collective, public-private partnership arrangements that could avoid the bad outcomes that are otherwise inevitable. In a nutshell, many of the practices now labeled examples of "collusion" or "conspiracy" should be legalized and then expanded as necessary to include government as a "coconspirator," or, more correctly, "coplanner." The first step is to outline why those engaged in competitive-bidding processes feel compelled to lie.

EVERYONE MUST LIE

When a public agency seeks approval for a project, it must estimate, as conservatively as possible, the final cost of the project, because the item might otherwise not be approved. This assertion is not easily subjected to an empirical test, because nobody can know in advance precisely what any project will cost, especially one using new technology. Further, no agency chief can publicly state at the outset that agency estimates are low. No estimate, therefore, can effectively be challenged.

As one example, take a recently completed sports arena in the New Jersey suburbs of New York City. A contractor in 1978 submitted the low bid of $54.75 million, and then announced, on the day bids were to be opened, that he had underestimated his costs by $8 million. The New Jersey Sports and Exposition Authority declared that it would hold the contractor to his estimate — a politically popular stance from which the Authority then had to retreat.

By 1980, costs stood at $80 million and, while final costs are as yet unknown, they will exceed $85 million.[12] In this instance, tragedies led to the approval of cost overruns: During the planning and construction phases of the New Jersey project, roofs on three other new sports arenas in the country collapsed, encouraging the local officials to make sure theirs was not the fourth to crumble.

Military cost overruns are widely publicized, but, as two principal analysts of former Defense Secretary McNamara have observed, overruns are common everywhere. As they put it, "Competition for the contract often drives contractors to bid on the basis of a target cost that is below what they actually expect the cost to be."[13] If a contractor seriously wishes to win a contract, he must make sure he underbids every likely competitor. Contractors and officials realize as much, but since neither can admit it, self-deception and mutual deception run wild. Technically, this is not lying, but, if Sissela Bok's ethical standard of "intentional deception" is brought to bear,[14] the actions amount to lying.

Cost overruns are not always feasible. In cases not involving new technology, in cases where contractors know that other contractors nearby perform similar work, and in cases where contractors know they will seek future business from the same agencies, there is pressure to submit bids that are within an agency's targeted costs, and to complete projects within those amounts. The only way to do this is to cheat by using illegally low-paid and untrained workers and shoddy materials, and then bribing inspectors. The risk is that expensive litigation may follow, and any contractor knows he may be forced to redo his work.

The most widespread forms of cheating may be the collusion and conspiracy contractors use to solve the inherent problems of competitive bidding. None of these forms, in all likelihood, is of recent invention, but prosecutors in the post-Watergate era vigorously ferret out white-collar crime. In the first three cases that follow, I emphasize the environmental factors that led private contractors to conclude they had little choice but to conspire among themselves because *some* form of regulation was necessary.

Case 1: The Electrical Companies

By October 1960, the federal government had indicted 29 corporations and 45 executives for conspiring to fix the prices of electrical equipment and machinery that ranged from small insulators to giant turbine generators and circuit breakers. In what remains the most famous case of its type, courts ultimately levied $1,924,500 in fines, with $810,000 being paid by General Electric (GE) and Westinghouse. Seven executives were jailed for 30 days, 25 others were given suspended sentences, and a number of others were demoted, forced into retirement, or given salary reductions. I am concerned here with how the companies "divided the business" of providing giant machinery to power companies, including the Tennessee Valley Authority.[15]

The manufacturers divided the country into four geographical regions, agreeing that only a few of them would submit bids for contracts in each region. One company submitted the low bid for one contract while others submitted higher bids, their positions shifting with each contract. GE executives kept records so that each company could verify that the business was being divided in accordance with the agreed market shares of 39 percent for GE, 35 percent for Westinghouse, 11 percent for I-T-E Circuit Breaker, 8 percent for Allis Chalmers, and 7 percent for Federal Electric. This required the companies to develop arcane signaling arrangements, such as rotating positions according to phases of the moon.

In passing sentence in 1961, the federal judge expressed the dominant opinion then and now:

> This is a shocking indictment of a vast section of our economy, for what is really at stake here is the survival of the kind of economy under which America has grown, the free enterprise system. The conduct of the corporate and individual defendants alike . . . has frequently mocked the image of the economic system of free enterprise which we profess to the country and destroyed the model which we offer today as a free world alternative to state control and eventual dictatorship.

Similarly, most would accept the conclusion of the then Attorney General Robert F. Kennedy: that the scheme was a "major and serious threat to democracy." Neither evaluation stands up.

To begin with, the industry had expanded beyond the plant capacity needed for the peacetime market, in part because government had authorized fast tax write-offs in order to develop the industrial-mobilization base needed in the event of war. Government, therefore had two policy objectives at stake, neither being clearly articulated.

The mobilization interest was to keep all companies in business, an interest seldom directly addressed. By definition, "reserve" plant capacity is not fully used in peacetime, so that some form of subsidy is needed if some plants are not to shut down. Had there been an accepted method by which government could have intervened in the contracting processes of local power companies, dividing the business as it did so, this would have been desirable. A second objective was antitrust purity. GE and Westinghouse probably had the ability to win most of the contracts, but this might have driven smaller competitors out of business. Meanwhile, the two giants had reason to fear antitrust intervention if their market shares continued to grow. To avoid this, GE and Westinghouse had to make sure they were not always successful. They thus conspired to *lose* business!

Power companies are separate from each other; they are regulated state-to-state by public-utility bodies. There was (and is now) no way for each company to know what all other companies were doing. Indeed, what was being planned in California was of little concern to a power company or a regulatory agency in New York. Each company and commission could seek only the best deal for meeting local needs. In responding to many agency requests, on the other hand, the manufacturers were in a quandary.

A small company (I-T-E) could have become the low bidder on many more contracts than it could have fulfilled, while GE and Westinghouse had to avoid total victory. It made little sense for every company to bid on every contract, but contracting agencies prefer this. And the agencies usually require bidders to post performance bonds proving they are serious. If corporate executives had reason to believe they risked prosecution, they also had reason to feel that planning was needed, so that collusion was the best of several bad choices. They had no reason at all to believe the random outcomes of separate bidding processes would make sense.

In light of what has been learned since, the companies can be said to have implicitly suggested a need for the orderly and systematic expansion of electrical power. Only nasty blackouts led to the establishment of a grid system that now allows for power transfer among individual companies and regions. Similarly, only a coordinated scheme, needed now as much as ever, can provide for sensible planning of power capacity, the industrial capacity needed to produce the machinery, the development (or closing down) of energy sources, and the building of reserve plant capacity if that is needed for defense purposes. Somebody had to plan, but the planners became the criminals.

I have presented this analysis to some economists and, as might be expected, they do not accept it. Their responses can be analyzed in ways applicable to the examples that follow:

First, the explanations of the electrical-company executives may have been only after-the-fact rationalizations of violations of law and company policies. Yet is it not understandable that executives charged with making decisions would avoid seeking written permission from corporate presidents for illegal decisions? This was a classic double bind, and it cannot be all that unusual among everyday managers. Alfred Sloan, who led General Motors to its dominant position, worked behind the scenes after World War II to make sure the Ford Motor Company, then in deep trouble, would not collapse, leading government to take it over so as to prevent a GM monopoly. Sloan worked with bankers to form a financial syndicate for use if Ford needed capital infusions, and also made it easy for GM executives to take jobs at Ford, which, at the time, had fewer professional managers than GM.[16] Had he publicly stated what he was doing, Sloan might have been labeled a conspirator.

Second, economists argue that competitive bidding is "socially productive" because it "drives price to marginal cost," and because it encourages "cost reduction or innovation." Closely analyzed, this is only a restatement of "consumer sovereignty." If a buyer, in this case government, can in principle achieve the lowest price through all-out competition among bidders, what is to be done with the redundant capacity after government makes its choices? In the jargon of economics, these are "economic externalities," costs for which the buyer is not responsible. But when governments are the approving authorities (as in the case of power companies and regulators), and when there are no other private customers for the output, then government itself creates the excess capacity. The "externalities" become societal "internalities" (waste), and society ultimately must absorb the costs. In this context, innovation and lower prices become unnecessary additional costs.

Lest any reader be misled, this analysis deals only with that part of the electrical conspiracy that managed the submission of sealed bids for equipment not sold in other ways. The managers who did the planning also sought to divide the market for a wide range of items sold in the normal manner. One analyst concludes that the conspiracy had little effect, in that the returns on capital and sales were lower during the conspiracy than before.[17] From my perspective, the conclusion is a bit different; even if this form of planning could not work well, it may have averted, for a time, huge overproduction and the immediate failure of one or more firms.

Case 2: Milk for the Kids

> LITTLE ROCK, Ark., Jan. 11 (1981) (AP) — Six years ago, a Parent-Teacher Association committee began checking the "junk food" content of cafeteria lunches and along the way discovered that all the bids for milk contracts were identical.
>
> Phyllis Brandon, the PTA's president, asked some questions that led to a state investigation, a Federal price-fixing lawsuit, and the largest antitrust settlement in Arkansas history.
>
> Merl Barns of the State Attorney General's office said the milk price investigation had uncovered an organized scheme among the dairies to fix prices to state institutions and wholesalers, and a more loosely organized price-fixing set-up for schools.
>
> Three dairies were indicted by a federal grand jury and pleaded no contest to criminal antitrust charges. Salesmen for two of the dairies served brief sentences in federal prison.
>
> In a decision Wednesday, Federal District Judge G. Thomas Eisele granted preliminary approval of the final and largest portion of a $2,424,000 settlement from the three dairies and a fourth one, all accused in a separate state civil suit. . . .
>
> [The three dairies] were Borden, Inc., Dean Foods, and Coleman Dairy, Inc. . . . No federal charges were filed against the Foremost-McKesson Dairy, but it was charged later in the state suit.[18]

In this case, the four established dairies cited above were deemed "fit" candidates for the milk contract. The school board decided to make the winner(s) responsible for the entire delivery system, including refrigeration units in the schools; 38 units were needed and, for any one dairy, the entire contract would have amounted to a 20-percent increase in business. What might have occurred under normal circumstances?

A winning contractor is often expected to be "fit, willing and able" to perform, immediately, and it is not uncommon to make awards only a few days or weeks in advance. Logically, each dairy should have geared up for a 20-percent increase in milk supplies, contracting with local farmers; the latter would have brought in more cows. Each dairy manager might have been required to increase plant capacity, and take on more trucks, drivers, and mechanics. Collectively, the four firms would have leased or purchased 152 expensive coolers, knowing that 114 of them would not be used. The school board, moreover, had announced that the contract would be opened each year for rebidding.

In a conversation with me, one dairy president asked, "What would I do with 38 coolers if I lost the contract after one year?"[19] The same question applied to all other equipment, cows, personnel, and new plant capacity. To school officials, of course, sealed bids were the norm, and it would have been thought improper to do anything else. Under these circumstances, dairy salesmen decided they must develop their own plan. By arranging to submit identical bids (note, again, that identical bids accomplished the normal market outcome of identical prices for all producers), they provided a basis for the school board to divide the business, thereby taking advantage of the distances between dairies and schools. This made it easy to compare performance records. Only the dairies were in a position to develop such a plan, one which could avoid other undesirable outcomes.

Had one dairy won the contract and then held it for many years, critics might have questioned its monopoly. Had one dairy won the contract, and had this raised its output to full plant capacity, it could not then have competed for new customers. Yet it seems reasonable that government contracts should not have the effect of making contractors less able to support themselves without the government business. And, of course, if a winning contractor had understated his costs, this might have led him to cheat on specifications.

The average citizen would assert that no dairy should feel compelled to cut corners on a school milk contract. A school official might suggest that, to ensure high-quality maintenance of coolers, a dairy should frequently inspect them, instead of waiting for breakdowns, and also might ask that any driver be given special training before entering a school's grounds. Yet a competitive-bidding process encourages contractors to risk the public's health and safety in order to meet the prices they offered under pressure. Many break-downs on school buses are traceable to such decision processes.

Case 3: Highway Robbery

As of mid-1982, the largest single antitrust investigation in the country's history was well underway: 160 cases had been brought in 11 states, alleging bid rigging and price fixing among highway-construction contractors. Of 17 other states in which grand juries thus far had been impaneled, only one had been given a clean bill of health. The deputy attorney general of the United States made clear what his department was about:

> We intend to seek out and prosecute those people who engage in hardcore antitrust violations like bid-rigging and price-fixing. . . . We're not talking about inadvertent conduct in an area where the law isn't clear. We're talking about widespread, collusive, criminal conduct that is literally stealing millions of hard-earned taxpayer dollars.[20]

In an intensive discussion of the investigations, the deputy attorney general was joined by the president of the National Asphalt Pavement Association (a contractors' trade group), an economist, and the special deputy attorney general of North Carolina. That state had recently made bid rigging punishable by up to five years in jail, a $100,000 fine for individuals, and million-dollar fines for corporations. The economist estimated that hundreds of millions of dollars had been lost to price fixing, the average overcharge being 10 percent.

Given the huge and expensive equipment used in highway con-struction, it is wholly illogical to believe that a large number of contractors can be uniformly ready to carry out each individual contract, especially in northern regions where construction seasons are limited by weather. The necessity to plan well in advance for the deployment of such equipment, and for the skilled people who operate it, makes it inevitable that some form of collective planning will take place. The president of the trade group pointed out that because some contractors have geographical advantages (proximity to contract sites), they are the logical companies to get those con-tracts; yet agency procedures require that "additional bids be called for." In some instances, bidders doubtless submit bids high enough to ensure they will lose, so that some forms of bid rigging are inevitable even without direct collusion.

One must also be cautious in accepting estimates of overcharging, although one need not assume the colluders charge only fair prices. If the industry is notorious for bid rigging, there is ample evidence of firms' cheating on specifications in order to complete projects without going over the amounts of money set aside for them. In April of 1982, for example, an uncompleted highway ramp collapsed in Indiana, killing 13 men, four of them carpenters. The representative of the local carpenters' union reported that carpenters he interviewed after the accident had been alarmed about the quality of the work being done, but had feared they would lose their jobs if they complained. The immediate cause of the collapse was cracks in concrete pads that crumpled in a chain reaction. Local authorities considered manslaughter charges, but the criminality may have been embedded in bidding processes. Had the winning firm, in order to gain the contract, understated its costs or, as is often the case, had it deliberately planned to pay illegally low wages while forcing workers to speed up? Governments routinely ignore such things because, as consumers, they have a vested interest in the lowest prices. They often do not hesitate to violate their own laws against low wages, simply by not bothering to enforce them.[21]

Case 4: Removing the Garbage

Trash removal is not of immediate global significance, but it is important to the quality of life. E. S. Savas, once a member of former New York Mayor John Lindsay's administration, later initiated, at Columbia University, the study of garbage removal in American cities. His evidence and views are noteworthy because he is a leading advocate of privatizing public-service delivery. His principal target for some years has been the "monopoly power" of municipal labor unions, especially the one which includes New York City's sanitation workers. Labeling this the "most severe management problem extant," Savas campaigned to have a substantial share of the city's garbage-removal function turned over, via competitive contracting, to private business. This, he asserted, would induce competition between public and private operators, thereby enabling officials to find ways of reducing costs.[22] The concept has made headway in New York City. In 1980 labor negotiations, the city threatened to experiment with private firms, whereupon the union accepted some new two-person trucks in place of traditional three-person vehicles. The new trucks, purchased through competitive bidding, were defective in construction and performance, and the ultimate costs have yet to be determined.[23]

Savas singled out Minneapolis as an example of how to improve efficiency.[24] His findings reinforced his belief that private operators functioning in a competitive environment are more efficient than monopolist public agencies. Some of his evidence, for Minneapolis and other cities, is open to question.[25] It appears that researchers underestimated the costs of supervising the contractors' performance, and also assumed that private workers enjoyed the same fringe benefits as municipal employees. Such questions ultimately will be significant in determining if private contractors invariably perform better, or merely are a contemporary example of how to use scab labor. I turn now to other aspects of the Minneapolis experience.

Prior to 1971, the city's Sanitation Division collected wet garbage from households, while private contractors were available, on an individual-contract basis, for rubbish and trash removal. Many citizens burned the trash on their premises, but a 1971 law ruled this out. City officials then decided to combine refuse collections, provoking a debate. City employees sought to expand the Sanitation Division, but the private firms argued that they should not be thrown out of business. A citywide committee recommended that the Sanitation Division be kept at the same size and serve some parts of the city, and that a consortium of the private firms be organized for serving the remainder of the city. Several dozen companies then formed the Minnesota Refuse Corporation, each receiving shares proportional to the number of residential customers it had previously served. The city negotiated a five-year contract with the consortium, insisting on a provision that called for the annual renegotiation of prices.

Savas praised the Minneapolis outcome, concluding that private-public competition had led to lower costs. He acknowledged the decision of the city to keep the old firms in business, rather than risk having a competitive contract won by a national agglomerate. Dedicated to classical principles, however, he concluded that "whether the public interest was best served by this process can be debated."[26] In extending his argument as to how to best handle garbage removal, and perhaps other functions as well, Savas developed an "ideal model" worth exploring.

Without using the phrase "natural monopoly," Savas admitted to important economies of scale:

> There are economies in having one truck collect refuse from every house on the block, and one would expect similar "economies of contiguity" in delivering newspapers, mail, milk, or campaign literature; in reading utility meters; or in mowing the postage-stamp lawns of suburban housing developments.[27]

He then recommended that large cities be divided into districts of no more than 50,000 population each, and that no contractor be awarded more than one district. A public agency would then remove the trash in one district, thereby minimizing the possibility of collusion among the private firms. The system could then be further purified by using a "process of periodic competition." Additionally, he noted:

> The ideal is to have many competing suppliers; award enough contracts both to avoid excessive reliance on a single supplier and to permit a significant fraction of the bidders to succeed in their quest, thereby encouraging the losers to try again next time; award few enough contracts so that the administrative burden is manageable; have the contracts small enough so that disaster does not strike someone who had a contract and then lost it; have the contracts large enough to allow economies of scale; and handle problems and pay bills promptly to keep suppliers interested in holding on to the business.[28]

If the Minneapolis approach worked, it was because government and the firms joined in a collective planning process that divided the business among firms then in existence. Assuming that government collected the data every year, there would be no need to annually reopen competitive bidding unless the city's own agency or some members of the consortium were performing in an inefficient manner (note, again, that a reopening for competitive bids could lead to understated costs). Conversely, it would have been almost impossible to achieve the Minneapolis results within Savas's prescribed "ideal."

Given a Minneapolis population of 434,000, eight districts would have been set up, seven of them for private firms. Given the rule that no firm could serve more than one district, the competitive-bidding process would have been ludicrous. If Savas is to be commended for recognizing the significance of "economics of contiguity" (something economists always avoid), his analysis falls a bit short. It makes more sense to interpret both his "ideal" and the Minneapolis experience as wholly justifiable designs of "legalized collusion."

FACING THE IMPLICATIONS

Desirable outcomes can be achieved only by abandoning economic theology in favor of collective partnership planning that includes the important parties. Such processes could not exclusively involve buyers and sellers, even when government is the buyer, for government is prone to accept or encourage starvation wages. There is nothing unusual about the suggestion, because the country has routinely used such approaches for high-priority projects. The Manhattan project of World War II was an example, but so was the peacetime effort to land men on the moon. The implications, however, are wide-ranging.

Some may argue that economy and efficiency were only secondary considerations in building nuclear bombs and launching space vehicles. Yet there is no reason to assume that these projects cost too much. To put it another way, why should the lives of those who build and test atomic bombs, or those who travel in space, be valued more highly than those who, for example, attended a Sunday dance at a Kansas City hotel in 1982? When overhead walkways collapsed and fell upon the dancers, who knew then that the cause was a decision to save money by weakening the supports that held up the concrete? While no manager intends to kill people, the unrelenting pressure to save money has the effect of compelling them to take chances that should not be taken.

The associated implication is that human behavior is traceable much more to the social environment than to heredity. The problem is not one of "born criminals" bent upon stealing from fellow citizens. If public officials lie to each other, and if contractors collude and cut corners, it is because the social environment leaves them with little other choice. The criminals are not those in jail for bid rigging, but the unknowing criminals who subscribe to the conventional economic wisdom. While these criminals deserve forgiveness, they can no longer command our allegiance.

It is widely accepted that when a government agency or a private firm asks for bids on a project, the agency or firm has a right to ask that the winning bidder give evidence of its competence and experience. This implies that except for wholly new projects, there cannot be an unrestricted right of entry. If, as this book argues, unrestricted competition is the only cause of a depression, then complete freedom of entry is the inevitable precursor of both an economic slump and a danger to the public's health and safety. Protection against new entry, then, is not a crime, but a necessary step to economic and physical health. Two further implications immediately follow.

If people are to be denied the unrestricted right to start up businesses, society as a whole becomes yet more responsible for acting as "employer of last resort." When President Reagan's chief economist recently announced that unemployment must remain at levels of 6-to-7 percent for the sake of the economy as a whole,[29] this was an implicit admission that up to 7 million citizens must perform the social duty of being jobless. The unemployed are not lazy, even if some of them actually might believe they prefer not to work. They are unemployed because they must be. If their purchasing power must be sustained, and Keynesianism is correct in this regard, this can work only within a larger scheme that regulates supply. Regrettably, proposals to privatize the delivery of public services are based upon the implicit hope that unemployment will remain high enough to force down public-sector wages. By the same token, there is no reason to assume that even a monopolist consciously limits output for the sake of maximizing profits. Antitrust cases are tried on the basis of assumptions, not fact, and the record does not even show that some monopoly power companies charged higher rates when they were not regulated.[30]

The purpose of this book is not to spell out in detail the precise form of regulation needed for each industry, but only to illustrate the need for regulation everywhere. The examples in this chapter show that what are now illegal forms of regulation indicate a needed form of regulation that should be legalized. The other side of the coin should be obvious. If regulation is necessary, it should follow that the attempt to completely deregulate any industry, by throwing that industry open to all-out competition, will of necessity lead to chaos, perhaps to widespread collapse, and danger to life and limb. The record is clear for those prepared to see it, and I turn now to a variety of examples.

NOTES

1. Martin Anderson, "Foreword," in E. S. Savas, *Privatizing the Public Sector: How to Shrink Government* (Chatham, N.J.: Chatham House, 1982), p. xi.

2. Ibid., p. 110.

3. Woodrow Wilson, "The Study of Administration," *Political Science Quarterly*, LVI, 4 (December 1941, reprinted from 1887), 485.

4. William A. Niskanen, Jr., *Bureaucracy and Representative Government* (Chicago: Aldine Atherton, 1971) esp. Chap. 20.

5. Savas, op. cit.

6. Vincent Ostrom, *The Intellectual Crisis in American Public Administration* (University, Ala.: University of Alabama Press, 1973), pp. 111-22.

7. Tullock credits the idea to James C. Miller. Gordon Tullock, *Private Wants and Public Means* (New York: Basic Books, 1970), pp. 112-13.

8. Robert Nozick, *Anarchy, State, and Utopia* (New York: Basic Books, 1974), pp. 18-21.

9. Robert Nisbet, *Twilight of Authority* (New York: Oxford, 1975), p. 278.

10. John E. Coons and Stephen D. Sugarman, *Education by Choice: The Case for Family Control* (Berkeley: University of California Press, 1978).

11. Domenick T. Armentano, *Antitrust and Monopoly: Anatomy of a Policy Failure* (New York: John Wiley, 1982), pp. 149-53.

12. *New York Times*, September 20, 1980, and telephone conversation with Office of Public Relations, New Jersey Sports and Exposition Authority, August 26, 1982.

13. Alain C. Enthoven and K. Wayne Smith, *How Much Is Enough? Shaping the Defense Program, 1961-1969* (New York: Harper & Row, 1971), pp. 239-40.

14. Sissela Bok, *Lying: Moral Choice in Public and Private Life* (New York: Vintage Books ed., 1978), chaps. 1-3.

15. This account is compiled from John M. Blair, *Economic Concentration: Structure, Behavior, and Public Policy* (New York: Harcourt Brace Jovanovich, 1972), pp. 576-80; John G. Fuller, *The Gentlemen Conspirators: The Story of the Price-Fixers in the Electrical Industry* (New York: Grove Press, 1962); and "Collusion Among Electrical Equipment Manufacturers," *Wall Street Journal*, January 10, 12, 1962, reprinted in Edwin Mansfield, *Monopoly Power and Economic Performance: The Problem of Industrial Concentration* (New York: Norton, 1968), pp. 89-96.

16. Peter F. Drucker, *Adventures of a Bystander* (New York: Harper & Row, 1978, 1979), pp. 291-93.

17. Armentano, op. cit., pp. 158-60.

18. *New York Times*, January 12, 1981.

19. Telephone interview, July 15, 1982.

20. Quotes are from "Highway Robbery," *The MacNeil-Lehrer Report*, June 23, 1982, Transcript # 1758. By September 4, 1982, 186 individuals and 156 corporations had been indicted; 131 individuals and 114 firms had entered guilty pleas; 16 individuals and ten firms had been found guilty after trials, with only nine individuals and six firms having been acquitted. *Washington Post*, September 4, 1982.

21. The story of the crumbling construction is from *Pittsburgh Press*, July 15, 1982. Workers on federally funded projects are required by law to be paid a "prevailing wage" (Davis-Bacon Act). Some believe this leads to wages that are too high, and occasional investigations indicate that many contractors routinely violate the law. Since the Labor Department has no budget for enforcement, little can be done. *Washington Post*, July 30, 1982.

22. E. S. Savas, "Municipal Monopoly," *Harper's*, December 1971, pp. 55-60; "Getting on Top of the Problem," *New York Times*, August 6, 1975.

23. *New York Times*, November 19, 1980, April 8, 1981.

24. E. S. Savas, "An Empirical Study of Competition in Municipal Service Delivery," *Public Administration Review* 37 (November/December 1977), 717-24.

25. Jacqueline DeLaat, "Contracting Out for Public Services: Some Unanswered Questions" (Doctoral diss., Graduate School of Public and International Affairs, University of Pittsburgh, 1982).

26. Savas, "An Empirical Study," p. 722.

27. Ibid., p. 718.

28. Savas, *Privatizing*, p. 152.

29. *New York Times*, November 22, 1982.

30. Armentano, op. cit., and George J. Stigler, "What Can Regulators Regulate? The Case of Electricity," in his *The City and the State: Essays on Regulation* (Chicago: University of Chicago Press, 1975), chap. 5.

5
The Ravages of Deregulation

Before looking at the results of deregulation, as those results have appeared in a number of industries, I wish to remove some of the confusion that surrounds the word "deregulation" itself. To begin with, there is the question of *social* deregulation and *economic* deregulation. In this country, liberals and conservatives tend to strongly disagree about how much social regulation of health and safety standards is needed, and the issue therefore gets much attention. Until she resigned in 1983 as director of the Environmental Protection Agency, for example, Ann McGill Burford was a favorite target of critics who argued that she and the Reagan administration were actively seeking to abolish or severely modify clean-air standards. When the subject is economic regulation, however, liberals and conservatives have recently agreed that the less we have of it, the better; and such industries as the airlines, trucking, buses, and even financial institutions have been deregulated, or subjected to "regulatory reform" having the same effect. Similarly, there has been no widespread opposition to the breaking up of American Telephone & Telegraph (AT & T), because almost everyone seems to despise a monopoly, even if it is performing well.

Indeed, agreement on the undesirability of economic regulation has been so widespread that the subject has moved into the realm often identified as the dominant view or even as common sense. A few years ago, just before Congress reformed the regulation of the trucking industry, James C. Miller III (then with the American Enterprise Institute and later the chairman of the Federal Trade

Commission in the Reagan administration) showed up on public television (in "The Advocates") as the debating partner of Senator Edward Kennedy, perhaps the most liberal of Democrats. The two of them painted a rosy picture of how much better things would be, once the trucking industry was released from the inefficient shackles that the Interstate Commerce Commission (ICC) had imposed upon truckers. Their principal opponent was a trucking-company executive who, identified as defending his vested interest, found himself facing a bipartisan coalition that reflected voting alignments in Congress. Had the issue been safety regulation, Kennedy would have been strongly proregulation, and Miller much more ready to let the market regulate itself.

This pattern has been widely repeated. On matters of economic deregulation, Ralph Nader and Milton Friedman have joined hands in attacking the ICC and the Civil Aeronautics Board (CAB), and so have Gerald Ford and Jimmy Carter. It seems to me, conversely, that if people of such diverse views are so strongly in agreement, common sense might well have given way to total confusion. As I shall seek to demonstrate, both liberals and conservatives overlook the important relationships between economic and social regulation. Simply put, social regulation of health and safety standards cannot be effective (or can become effective only at very high costs) unless it is accompanied by economic regulation; in an environment of all-out competition, social regulation cannot work well.

Second, in asserting that I seek to demonstrate this connection, I acknowledge what many analysts of public policy choose to over-look: We all should admit that it is virtually impossible to scientif-ically prove any proposition having to do with public policy. There is little choice but to collect the available data associated with a real situation, and compare those data with the imaginary data of a hypothetical situation. Those who now defend the deregulation of the airline industry, for example, often make such assertions as: "If regular coach fares have risen since deregulation in 1978, the fares have risen more slowly than they would have risen under continued CAB fare regulation." The only fact is that such fares have risen, but whether the fares would have risen more or less in some different set of circumstances depends solely upon any observer's judgment as to the cause-effect relationships among deregulation, profits, and prices. Similarly, attacks on such formerly accepted monopolies as AT & T must begin with the assumption that any real monopoly always is more inefficient than a hypothetical free market. The upshot is that any argument must be based upon theory, not upon fact, and the available data are always interpreted from the particular observer's perspective.

A third item of confusion to clear away is that economic deregulation can have meanings that, at first glance, appear wholly contradictory. When someone advocates deregulation of oil and natural-gas prices, the argument is that regulation has kept such prices "artificially low," thereby removing incentives for exploration. In principle, the promise of higher prices and profits leads to new discoveries of oil and gas that, in turn, lead to lower prices for consumers. The supporters of airline and trucking deregulation, conversely, argued that the CAB and the ICC had kept fares and rates "artificially high" because, in principle, only a free market can provide consumers with the lowest prices and greatest benefits. Taken together, these arguments can indeed confuse even the citizen who follows them every day, but this is what happens when anyone follows the twists and turns of economic theology. If oil prices are to rise under conditions of deregulation, this might well prevent reductions in airline fares, but the typical economist then would insist that only a free-market price is wholly legitimate. In some of the examples I shall cite, deregulation has led to lower prices (for at least some buyers) but, in other examples, prices have rapidly escalated. I shall argue that deregulation doesn't work well, whether the outcome is collapsing prices or runaway price rises.

Finally, deregulation can occur in a variety of ways. While the word is often associated with the removal of a regulatory agency's authority to set prices and control entry into an industry, other actions can have the same effect. As indicated earlier, the rebuilt industries of Europe and Japan, and the new industries in developing countries, have effectively removed the self-regulation that sustained American prosperity for so long a time following World War II. This country's communications system has been deregulated by the agreement — initiated by the Justice Department and approved in a federal court — to break up AT & T. A bipartisan agreement to encourage all-out competition among banks, by deregulating interest rates, probably has done more to keep interest rates high than the Federal Reserve Board could have dreamed of doing. Yet another example is professional sports, where a series of court decisions has led to all-out bidding wars for the services of athletes, but with new forms of necessary economic regulation now beginning to emerge. In examining what has happened in these industries, I shall be pursuing a common set of themes.

Whatever form it takes, economic regulation remains more the norm than the exception. If, for example, all government interventions, beginning with price supports and the buying of surpluses, were to be wiped out in agriculture, a collapse in farm production might again produce widespread starvation and food riots. If all the other forms of protection were abandoned, as many economists would prefer, what in the early 1980s is a serious depression would become a national disaster. This may happen even if things stay as they were early in 1983, because the global banking system was sufficiently deregulated to be poised on the brink of collapse. In the examples that follow, I will indicate how particular snippets of economic theory, as they have been applied to individual industries, have ruined the industries and added to analytical confusion. I begin with the airlines.

AIRLINES: EMPTY-SEAT PRICE WARS

Before the airlines were deregulated in 1978, a passenger seeking a flight from New York to Los Angeles could choose from among American, Trans World Airlines (TWA), and United. In choosing one of the three, the traveler left the other two with empty seats. The three firms scheduled their flights at about the same time, in order to meet peak travel demand. Had they not done this, one or more of them might have been found guilty of failing to provide enough flights to meet demands of public convenience and necessity — the standard test for a public utility. Invariably, this left many seats empty, but this must happen if passengers are to exercise their consumer sovereignty by choosing one seller over others. Because the CAB was compelled by law to promote competition, it was in no position to command airlines to limit the number of flights. The long-term problem of the airlines, then, was empty seats, especially on such high-density routes (city pairs) as New York-Los Angeles.*

---

*Ironically, some of the most highly traveled routes produced the greatest number of empty seats, because more airlines competed for the same passengers.

This was not a small problem, especially during periods of technological change. If three competitors all buy larger and more efficient planes, with each new plane being able to carry, say, 350 passengers instead of the 150 carried on each old plane, the number of empty seats will drastically increase unless one or more of the competitors drops out. This problem became extraordinarily troublesome from time to time, so much so that in the early 1970s, the CAB finally decided that it could properly ask American, TWA, and United to agree among themselves to restrict the number of flights on the New York-Los Angeles route (and some other routes as well), for the sake of reducing the number of empty seats, thereby helping the airlines to recover from badly sagging profits and, after the oil embargo of 1973, to conserve fuel. After all, if three planes are used to carry passengers who could travel in a single plane, the result is inefficient and wasteful.

Using a version of common sense foreign to economics, the CAB's action was wholly justifiable. Even Judge Breyer, who assisted Senator Kennedy in developing the deregulation legislation, acknowledges that by the late 1960s, the combination of large new aircraft and high schedule frequencies left the airlines with 60 percent of their seats empty; and that a financial return of 4.3 percent on total investment was much too low. He even complains that "the CAB found it impossible to convince the domestic carriers to agree to compete less by limiting the number of flights."[1] The CAB concluded in 1975 that the agreements were unlawful, and canceled them. Breyer, now criticizing the CAB for allowing illegal agreements at all concludes that "legality aside, their wisdom was highly debatable."[2] The ardent deregulator, it appears, ultimately must reassert theological purity, even after acknowledging that the CAB did only what it should have done earlier. In common with other critics of the CAB and the industry, Breyer finds that wasteful "service" competition had replaced efficient "price" competition. The most widespread attack has been upon such "frills" as gourmet meals, liquor, wide seats, in-flight movies and live entertainment, and too many flights. All these were caused by the "rigid pricing rules" of the CAB, says Breyer, in a book advertised by its publisher as "the bible of regulatory reform."[3] The attack upon service

---

Veteran passengers may remember how TWA advertised that "the seat next to you is always empty."

competition is so misdirected that its survival is a testimony to the absurdities of economic thought.

There is no doubt that service competition is wasteful, but it has long been common among large firms seeking to maintain or improve market shares. Each of four oil companies, for example, may keep a service station open all night at the same street corner, to keep abreast of its competitors, even though each station may have only a handful of customers late at night. This cannot be blamed upon a regulatory agency, just as nonfunctional design frills on automobiles (tail fins) were traceable to competition, not to regulation. In the glory days of self-regulation, of course, oil companies and auto manufacturers were able to set prices high enough to cover the high costs of service competition. What the critics hoped would occur, upon deregulation of the airlines, was some combination of the following: more competing carriers on every important route; all-out price competition to lower fares and encourage more people to fly; and flight frequencies more closely aligned with travel demand.

With deregulation now the law of the land, there no longer are three airlines competing on transcontinental routes, but seven, the struggle having been joined by Capitol, Eastern, Pan American, and World Airways (at last count). The passenger who chooses one must leave six seats empty and, in the mysterious world of economics, the increase from two to six empty seats is labeled "greater efficiency." The airlines, forced into all-out competition, were turned loose to fly any routes they wished. With seven firms competing on a route where only four used to compete, the total number of flights could only increase, thereby making service competition more widespread than before. In trying to fill seats to get at least some return, the airlines had to engage in all-out price wars. Classic competition did indeed take over, with an ever-increasing overproduction of seats, many of them being sold at ridiculously low discount prices. Discounting became so intense that World Airways, one of the small firms thought to be the beneficiaries of deregulation, asked the CAB to reassert its authority by setting a price floor that would at least cover demonstrable operating costs.[4]

The advent of deregulation brought about an initial upsurge in air travel, especially on the vacation routes, as customers flocked to take advantage of bargain fares. The profits of the scheduled carriers reached an all-time high of $1.4 billion in 1978, and even airline presidents began to believe that a magic formula had been discovered. Many of them began to add all sorts of new facilities, and a few (Braniff being the most conspicuous example) piled new route upon new route in an attempt to expand as quickly as possible. The champions of deregulation were convinced they had been proved correct, and Milton Friedman quickly pronounced the new policy a "dramatic success."[5] Some wondered if all the new discount passengers (paying less than cost) would become frequent travelers, and the answer was soon forthcoming.

Indeed, 1979 was the first full year of deregulation, and profits fell by 80 percent, to $199 million. This was followed in 1980 by losses of $222 million, making it, until then, the worst single year in the history of the industry.* In a desperate attempt to offset some of the losses incurred in price wars on vacation routes, companies raised regular coach fares to unbelievable heights. By mid-1981, just before the strike by the government air-traffic controllers, the round-trip, transcontinental coach fare had jumped to almost $1,000. The advocates of deregulation, including most of the major media, pointed to discount fares as evidence of success, resolutely ignoring financial losses and extremely high fares on nonvacation routes, and also overlooking the withdrawal of major airlines from a number of smaller cities.

The supporters of deregulation have attributed the financial woes of most large carriers to some combination of rising fuel prices, deteriorating economic conditions, and managers who had learned bad habits during the long period of CAB protection against competition. This accords with the standard economic view: that because perfectly free markets are beyond criticism, a policy of deregulation could only have solved old problems without causing new ones. The characteristics of airline systems are not all that unique, but to mention some of them is to show how abstract economic theology, literally applied, causes many more problems than it solves.

---

*New records are now set every year. In 1981 losses soared to $421 million, only to jump to more than $700 million in 1982. Preliminary data for the first quarter of 1983 indicate that it was the worst three-month period in history. Data are available from the Air Transport Association in Washington, D.C.

What Is an Airline?

Proponents of deregulation argue that the industry is "structurally competitive," in that it is both easy and desirable for new entrants to begin operations:

> The theoretical argument for the efficiency of deregulated airline markets is extremely powerful. The airline industry appears to conform closely to the necessary conditions for price competition: no significant economies of scale, fairly elastic demand, relative difficulty of coordinating pricing and output policies (that is, collusion), and, in the absence of controls, relative ease of entry and exit.[6]

The true believers gave much attention to the experience of small intrastate airlines in California and Texas. Operating in only a few city-pair markets (e.g., Los Angeles-San Francisco, and Dallas-Houston), they offered lower fares, and appeared to demonstrate that all one needs to operate an airline is one or two planes and a handful of pilots and mechanics. Unless passengers are to change planes at every stop, however, city-pair markets must overlap and this, in turn, must lead to relatively large and fixed systems. The airlines have had to develop the most extensive computer facilities anywhere outside the U.S. government;[7] hence "ease of entry and exit" is a foolish notion. When this expansion becomes truly long-range, airlines must have mechanics, relief crews, and other facilities at many locations around the world, and impressive scale economies then emerge.

Long-haul transportation systems have always operated as the equivalent of continuous conveyors. If a bus, truck, train, or plane is to keep moving, it is necessary to change drivers, engineers, or pilots along the way. The vehicle continues on, the operators resting until it is time for them to replace other operators of later vehicles. To achieve the greatest efficiency, an airline must indeed have many planes and employ perhaps six-to-eight complete flight crews per plane, and comparable numbers of mechanics and other servicing personnel. To do anything else is to be economically wasteful and also to incur safety risks (as would be the case if crews did not rest properly). I outline such phenomena because while they are familiar to logisticians, they seem unknown to economists. Contrary to conventional wisdom, air-transport operations have enormous potential for economies of scale, the best (if an extreme) example being the Berlin airlift.

What about "Cross-Subsidy?"

An individual who lives on the outskirts of a city cannot afford to pay the full economic costs of public transportation, yet policy-makers may decide that bus service should be available there. Some of the costs of that individual's travel are paid by passengers who ride on high-density routes. Historically, for example, the fares of passengers flying from Harrisburg to Peoria have been "subsidized" by those traveling from New York to Washington. If a regulatory agency directs an airline to serve both routes, the airline will not be able to precisely determine how to allocate costs, especially since airline travel is highly cyclical. If the attempt is made to relate fares to costs, however, the Harrisburg-Peoria passenger may be charged a fare that is high enough to prevent all but the most affluent passengers from flying at all. If decisions are made solely on the basis of the costs and prices in each discrete market, airlines are unlikely to provide any service at all to small communities, and some observers believe all such decisions should be left solely to the market. After all, why should I pay the same price for mailing a letter within a city as a farmer pays for mailing his letters?

The new entrants, sometimes known as "upstart airlines," do not choose Harrisburg-Peoria and similar routes. They are natu-rally attracted to high-density routes and, with no responsibilities to serve small communities, they can minimize their expenses and offer lower fares. The policy of deregulation simultaneously per-mitted new airlines to begin operations wherever they chose, and made it difficult for the established companies to abandon all the small cities they had been directed to serve. Obviously, this exacer-bated the financial problems of the old companies; they had to meet the lower fares of new competitors, but this took away the revenues they had used to offset the losses on low-density routes. Even worse, all-out competition produced an upside-down version of cross-subsidy. In the past few years, tourists have gotten most of the bargains, but wholly at the expense of those who must fly for business reasons and those living in small cities. Assuming business travel can be important to the economy, and assuming that those who can afford to spend a week at a resort should pay reasonable fares for their travel, this reverse cross-subsidy may be the most unjustifiable subsidy of all. The most equitable fare system would be one based upon mileage, but such a system cannot be sustained without economic regulation.

Have Old Airlines Discovered New Efficiencies?

There is little doubt that deregulation has encouraged all airlines to cut costs as much as possible, but, as I shall suggest below, cost reductions may have increased safety risks. One important approach to improved efficiency, however, has been increased reliance upon "hub-spoke" operations. An airline can consolidate its crews and facilities at one major airport, operating most of its flights on an out-and-back basis. The classic example has been Delta's focus on Atlanta; and Federal Express has made its operations efficient by routing through Memphis all the cargo it carries. While "hub-spoke" operations can be efficient for any one carrier, this system as a whole becomes inefficient when direct competitors use it.

American Airlines chose to consolidate its operations at Dallas Airport, while United uses Chicago as a major hub. Both airlines fly between Dallas and Chicago, American flying Dallas-New York and United flying Chicago-New York. In the desperate attempt to fill more seats, United offered passengers a lower fare for taking a circuitous connecting route, Dallas-Chicago-New York, than American charged for a nonstop Dallas-New York flight. A passenger willing to spend three extra hours (some of it in flight, some on the ground in Chicago) could save perhaps $40. As more passengers chose to do this, United added flights to accommodate them, taking passengers from American. The result was a system in which passengers were charged less for flying greater distances, thus making the overall transportation system much more inefficient. Furthermore, unnecessary circuitous routings overload the air traffic control system while needlessly exposing passengers to added risks, since most accidents occur on landings and takeoffs. Economic analysts could not understand why, if American had become so successful at consolidating its operations in Dallas, it continued to lose money; but the answer was the same for American as for other companies: Taken to its logical extreme, competing "hub-spoke" systems promote inefficient overuse of circuitous routing, and costs continue to climb while income declines.

In late April of 1983, most major airlines quietly converted their regular coach fares to a mileage-based system, deciding that "hub-spoke" price wars had gotten out of hand. When this was written (May 1983), United and American once again charged identical fares between Dallas and New York, thereby removing any incentive for passengers to fly via Chicago rather than nonstop. What remained an open question was whether someone, in government or elsewhere, would decide that the new mileage-based fare structures were the result of illegal collusion. Yet it would seem reasonable and logical to prohibit one airline (United, in this example) from charging a lower fare for a circuitous route than a competitor (American) charges for a nonstop flight. As I shall indicate below, safety issues are connected with such examples.

The list of questions could be extended, but I shall turn instead to one important event that, while given extraordinary public attention, was not perceived as demonstrating the silliness of airline deregulation. When the government's air-traffic controllers went on strike in 1981, they doubtless believed that the Reagan administration would have to bargain with them if the air-travel system was not to be shut down. Their mistake was not in believing that the president would bargain, but, rather, in assuming that all, or even most, of the flights then operating were needed. When Secretary of Transportation Drew Lewis quickly installed a somewhat makeshift air-traffic-control system, he simultaneously restricted flights in and out of 22 major airports. In some instances, flights were reduced by as much as 50 percent, and many believed that with such low flight frequencies, passengers by the thousands, or even the hundreds of thousands, would be unable to take trips already planned, or would be stranded in places around the country and even around the world. However, except for some relatively minor dislocations at the beginning, air travel was hardly disrupted at all.

The proponents of deregulation have said little about the controllers' strike, because only one conclusion is possible: The overcapacity in the industry, represented by too many flights and too many empty seats, was so great that the government could get along quite well by replacing more than 10,000 controllers with only a fraction of that number. In the freely competitive airline market of 1981, it was wholly irrelevant to determine which airlines were more or less efficient than others. With all the old airlines and a number of new ones competing for the same passengers, the overall air-travel system was inefficient virtually beyond comprehension. Indeed, the imposition of flight restrictions probably enabled some carriers to avoid bankruptcy for the time being. The failure of Braniff, similarly, was more an indication of overcapacity than of managerial inefficiency.

The final point to be raised about airline deregulation is the relationship of economic and safety regulation. Because airline accidents are relatively few in number when compared with the total number of flights, statistical data are not wholly reliable trend indicators. There often have been some categories of airlines, however, that were not placed wholly within the CAB regulatory regime, and the record is clear that these airlines always had higher accident rates than did fully regulated carriers.[8] The small commuter airlines, similarly, became a focus of National Transportation Safety Board (NTSB) interest in 1979-80, because those deregulated companies were suffering many accidents as they expanded operations to replace established airlines then withdrawing from small cities.

In a thoughtful study, J. M. Ramsden developed the concept of "subtle corporate incapacitation," to describe what can happen as these competitive pressures take hold:

> The airline industry knows that safe airlines are financially strong airlines. Financial weakness rarely affects safety directly. Even "cowboy" operators, of which there will always be some, know that crashes hurt business — not to mention their own necks. Owners who "cut corners" — who tear out Technical Log defect reports, instead of fixing them, and who push pilots to carry Class A ("no-go") snags or to exceed duty times — are the cowboys who have always flown that way, and got away with it. . . .
>
> An operator enters the business with a loan, perhaps from a bank or tour company. Ticket deposits at the start of the season help him finance the operation, including staff wages. The aircraft, rent, maintenance and fuel bills, airport landing fees and so on, down to the office cleaners, will be fully paid at the end of the season at the latest. All is well while business is good. But if traffic falls short of expectations, working capital has to be raised on the more speculative expectation of the following year's traffic.
>
> Now the bank or tour operator starts to demand a bigger say in the running of the airline in which it has so much at risk. It calls for cuts here and cuts there, with little understanding of the operation.

The staff, especially pilots and engineers, sense trouble. Morale declines. Management becomes more and more evasive and preoccupied with the commercial crisis, leaving the safety professionals increasingly unsettled about their problems. Staff start to leave, and management refuses to replace them. As a result heads of departments such as flight operations and maintenance come under ever greater stress. Maintenance, crew-roster and training schedules and records become disordered. Accounts fall further and further behind. A general atmosphere of shambles pervades the operation. Morale and discipline, on which safety so much depends, decline. Auditors, creditors and government safety inspectors become less and less tolerant.

This is the atmosphere in which financially weak airlines can become vulnerable to accidents. . . .[9]

The airlines were under extreme pressure to cut costs before deregulation became law, because the drive for deregulation dates at least from the mid-1970s. While direct cause-effect relationships cannot be proved, I will use three specific examples of what can occur.

First, the DC-10 crash in Chicago (1979) was viewed at first as yet another problem for an aircraft that had developed a dubious reputation for safety. It turned out, however, that the airline (American) had decided to save money on engine inspections by removing in one operation the jet engines and their supporting pylons. The procedure was not recommended by the manufacturer, and the fact that the simplified procedure had created a dangerous condition was not discovered until the crash had occurred. The extensive litigation associated with that crash has yet to be completed, but reports indicate that most of the settlement will come from the airline.

Second, in the crash at Washington National Airport in the winter of 1981-82, deregulation can properly be labeled a contributing factor. When the National Transportation Safety Board concluded its investigation, it did not mention deregulation, but it said enough to make the case. The NTSB pointed out that the pilots had had little experience with winter flying weather. This can happen when a small airline, using young nonunion pilots, suddenly expands its operations into geographical regions with which crew members are unfamiliar. There is much to be said for having airlines remain on fixed routes, so that training programs can incorporate institutional memory data, and pilots become conversant with the problems particular airports face in particular weather conditions. The NTSB also noted a lack of coordination between the airline that had de-iced the aircraft (American), and the airline flying it (Air Florida) – an example of the half-baked cartelization ("renting" a mechanic) that has increased since deregulation. Worse yet, American did not fly that type of aircraft and had no operating manual for servicing it. The NTSB noted, moreover, that the pilots on too many airlines, including that one, had been trained to avoid the use of maximum engine power because this increased maintenance costs, implying that the use of full power may have saved this aircraft and its passengers.

Third, while some questioned Braniff's quick expansion, *Fortune* concluded in early 1979 that almost everyone conceded that the company had "one of the smartest management groups in the industry." But it was not long until Braniff was fined heavily by the Federal Aviation Administration (FAA) for shoddy maintenance practices – an indication that hasty expansion had led to corner cutting. Until the company declared bankruptcy in 1982, there were periodic reports of its financial difficulties (it was not the only company so mentioned, of course), and now evidence emerges that tension was rife in the company. The *Texas Monthly* reports that Braniff's president, Harding Lawrence, had repeatedly tossed tantrums on Braniff flights; some examples are given:

- upset at being given the wrong food, he slammed his fist into the plate, splattering food throughout the first-class section;
- annoyed at some other happening, he shouted profanely at the crew, threatening to fire them all;
- he smashed a wine glass into his tray, leading other first-class passengers to leave the section;
- he overturned a champagne bucket;
- upset that his food had gotten cold, he dumped the tray onto the lap of a stewardess;
- he repeatedly called executives at 3 a.m. to berate them about their (and the airline's) failures.[10]

Are we to believe that the management of American Airlines is comprised of evil and unscrupulous individuals, that Air Florida is thoroughly slipshod and careless, and that the president of Braniff was psychologically unstable; or does it make more sense to conclude that a desperately competitive environment pushed the companies into "subtle corporate incapacitation?" I choose the latter.

The usual argument is that economic and safety regulation can be separated from each other, and that the removal of economic regulation does not alter the responsibility of the FAA to maintain safety standards in the airline industry. As in other instances, this is an organizationally naive argument. When large firms have consolidated training and maintenance facilities, it is relatively easy for safety inspectors to visit those facilities, examine records, and spot-check aircraft and pilots. The larger the firm, the more necessary it is to use standardized procedures that cannot easily be changed, so that inspectors know that a spot-check gives them an accurate picture. The fewer the number of firms, the fewer the number of inspectors required. As the number of firms increases, more and more inspectors are needed, and effective safety enforcement requires higher and higher expenditures by enforcement agencies.

While this relationship between economic regulation and safety regulation is often denied, the leading advocate of airline deregulation has admitted its existence. Alfred E. Kahn served as CAB chairman during the Carter administration, shepherding deregulation through Congress as he did so. More recently, he wrote in favor of continuing a regulation he had instituted as CAB chairman, one requiring airlines to compensate passengers bumped from flights after being given confirmed reservations:

> When consumers are inadequately informed, competition may take the form of providing adulterated or unsafe products, with the least scrupulous among the competitors forcing the more scrupulous to cut corners as well. It shouldn't be surprising that many ethical business people themselves are eager to have the government set limits on this kind of competition.[11]

If all competitors must lower standards in order to compete, it is of little significance to buyers whether some producers may be more genetically dishonest than others. The more accurate judgment would be that it is the competitive environment itself that compels firms to cut corners, and that cost cutting inevitably must affect safety. When firms are losing money, managerial judgment becomes distorted. Airline passengers, moreover, submit many more complaints about the upstart airlines than about more established carriers.[12] Many complaints may refer to quality of service, not to safety, but the average passenger may not be equipped to see the connection between poor quality and safety risks. If deregulation has thrown the airline industry into financial chaos, safety problems must lie ahead.

At one level of analysis, only theory can be a wholly reliable guide. The upstart airlines, none of them unionized, compel their pilots to fly many more hours per month than do older airlines, and this usually involves a higher ratio of landings and takeoffs to flying hours. Nobody can know for sure when fatigue becomes a major problem, but there is little reason to experiment day after day to find out how many hours can be flown before accidents occur. When unionized pilots complain that safety ultimately must suffer, they are dismissed as a "special interest," but the record supports them on two counts: When economic regulation is absent or ineffective, there are more accidents. Furthermore, until fuel prices became a problem in the 1970s, the airlines, and electric-power companies as well, had experienced "decreasing real prices over a span of many years."[13] Even though CAB regulation did not meet *my* standards for regulation, it served consumers rather well and, given the reasonable prices and the lack of high profits, deregulation was instituted purely on theoretical grounds.

At another level, however, data can be found to support the argument that deregulation is an abysmal failure. The CAB has monitored important financial indicators for years but, since the agency is itself scheduled for abolition in 1984, data soon may be unavailable. For that reason, it may be desirable to highlight some of the indicators for the sake of making a historical record. As the charts in the Appendix to this chapter show, the airline industry is in very bad shape. Given the losses outlined above, this is no surprise, but the advocates of deregulation prefer to ignore such things. They are content to argue, as Kahn does, that because the airlines filled 59 percent of their seats in 1982 (as opposed to an average of 52 percent in the 1970-75 period), this proves that "deregulation has forced them to use their equipment more efficiently."[14] No mention is made here of how price wars and overuse of connecting flights can produce misleading figures. The data in the Appendix seem more illustrative, as do various reports that airlines have been forced to cancel or substantially delay the buying of new and more fuel-efficient planes.[15]

TRUCKS: CHAOS ON THE ROADS

The *Washington Post*, a strong supporter of economic deregulation, indicated in 1982 just how powerful economic theology can be, by highlighting the experience of one independent trucker. As the reporter put it, "deregulation means he doesn't have to take the backroads from Dallas to San Francisco anymore." Prior to the "regulatory reform" of 1980, this trucker had to make "under-the-table payments" to get loads because he did not have Interstate Commerce Commission authority to haul loads on that route. The theme of the article was that while the trucker and various shippers had earlier engaged in illegal collusion, this was a morally correct reaction to the legalized improprieties of the ICC and the Teamsters Union. The trucker's words were quoted with implied approval:

> I'm real pleased they finally woke up and put this thing on a competitive basis instead of letting the chosen few have all the legal authority to haul goods. Now we are out there legally grabbing a piece of the action for ourselves too. The real reason they're screaming is that they've had a monopoly jerked right out from under them.

An accompanying article quoted at length from the observations of William Ris, transportation counsel for the Senate Commerce Committee, who asserted that "deregulation will ultimately benefit the industry," but only after "a period of consolidation . . . and more individual bankruptcies that would not have taken place without deregulation." Also quoted was congressional testimony by an official of the American Trucking Association, who noted that 144 carriers had left the industry since 1980, and that 90 others (representing $2 billion in annual revenues and more than 42,000 jobs) were close to bankruptcy.[16] One example was Hemingway Transport, which bought in 1979 a new fleet of trucks at a cost of $79 million, which required annual loan payments of $4 million. Its president insisted that without substantial concessions from unions, it could not stay in business.[17] Meanwhile, the Teamsters were said to have lost 21 percent (63,000) of their members.[18]

The trucking industry is a classic case of how policy decisions must be made on the basis of theory because virtually no comprehensive data are available. One researcher recently reported that more than 83 percent of the ICC-regulated trucking companies gross less than $1 million a year and, by law, do not have to file annual reports with the agency; the ICC has no way of knowing if they are still in business. Further, the ICC does not require carriers to report if they are leaving the industry. In checking still further, the researcher concluded that bankruptcy figures supplied by the Teamsters, the American Trucking Association, and the Regular Common Carrier Conference are all open to question and appear inaccurate.[19] A brief historical summary may show why there are so little data.

When the ICC began regulating trucks in 1935, 28,000 existing firms were "grandfathered" into the regulated system, but about 40 percent of the industry was exempted from regulation (in particular, those hauling farm produce). Through mergers and other changes, the regulated firms had dwindled to 15,000 in the 1970s. On high-volume eastern routes, 20-to-30 competitors fought over each route, the top four usually accounting for 50-to-60 percent of the business. In the West, an average of a dozen companies served each major route, the top four handling about 90 percent of the business. Before deregulation, the best example of a high-volume route and of all-out competition was that of the 92 firms competing for New York-Boston shipments.[20]

Because no single agency could carefully have examined the records of so many firms before setting prices, ratemaking was turned over to collective bureaus financed and operated by the industry. The ICC had authority to reverse such decisions, but it seldom did. As to the bureaus, they were in no position to collect detailed operating data, because each firm treats its data as proprietary information not to be released to competitors. I can testify from experience that it is virtually impossible to discover precisely how much empty space is on each truck engaged in Less-Than-Truckload (LTL) operations.

To the advocates of deregulation, even the presence of 92 firms on a route made things only "potentially competitive," because the work of the ratemaking bureaus seemed to be only "ratefixing by cartel."[21] The critics argued that, like the airlines, "service competition [was] excessive" in trucking, and that "more frequent service" caused firms to "drive trucks that are inefficiently empty."[22] The proposed solution was deregulation, for this would presumably lead to less empty space. Yet it would appear that when there were "only" 92 companies on the New York-Boston route, a shipper choosing one would leave 91 others with empty space; and that if still more firms joined the chase, this would produce still more unused space.

One of the most curious arguments in favor of deregulation was that the ICC had unfairly restricted some trucking firms to one-way hauling, permitting them to move freight from A to B, but not from B to A. The problem of "empty backhaul" was mentioned again and again, and Breyer approvingly cites a study that estimated that 38 percent of general-freight vans had to return empty because of ICC restrictions.[23] Individual truckers were brought forth to testify that their economic freedom was being unjustifiably abridged. Yet the argument not only assumed that much freight was not being moved at all (did the critics believe that if the 38 percent of trucks that were previously empty were filled, all the others would remain filled also?), but ignored built-in imbalances (because Washington is not a manufacturing city, much more is shipped in than out). Because virtually everyone accepted the theology, however, reform (deregulation) was a foregone conclusion once it was introduced in Congress.

Political imagery was and is all important. The independent owner-operator has become a folk hero. He is pictured as a "lonesome cowboy" of the highways, listening to music written for his ears, keeping in touch with fellow operators via CB radio, and, most important of all, keeping tabs on police who might disapprove of high-speed driving. No individual better fits the image of the "little guy" trying to get ahead by competing against the "big fellows." No union has a worse reputation than the Teamsters and, indeed, its former president has been convicted of seeking to bribe a key senator when reform legislation was before him. And, even if not yet abolished, the rate bureaus fit the image of greedy conspirators who overcharge shippers and, in turn, consumers.

The deregulation proponents acknowledge a huge trucking overcapacity in the 1930s, but they ascribe this wholly to general economic conditions, ignoring the likelihood that even under the best of circumstances, 28,000 trucking firms would not have been profitable. Because the deregulators do not acknowledge the link between economic and safety regulation, they have dismissed important evidence. A professor at the Harvard Business School undertook, a few years ago, a massive study of trucking but, in seeking out drivers, had little choice but to leave questionnaires at truck stops, hoping to get something of a representative sampling of how the industry operated. The nature of the industry is such that truly scientific data are impossible to collect — leaving the advocates of deregulation to argue that the professor's evidence was questionable. He found that, compared with regulated truckers, unregulated operators have many more serious accidents, more frequently violate driving-time limits (ten hours per shift), make many more false entries in the logbooks they must keep, and collect many more moving violations. His conclusions, while gently stated, were clear enough, and their dismissal by legislators and other policy-makers was inexcusable:

> The observations of experienced motor carrier managers that there is substantially better compliance with safety and operating rules in the ICC-regulated sector were confirmed. Compliance . . . [was] highest among company employees in the highly regulated common-carrier segment and lowest in the exempt segment. Is the relationship between economic regulation and safety compliance causal? Economic regulation does result in larger carriers than exist in the exempt area. Motor-carrier managers believe and act as if the ICC is fulfilling its mandate to ensure that carriers under its jurisdiction are fit, willing, and able, . . . [although] it is difficult to confirm a causal relationship. . . .[24]

If nobody can prove the connection exists, plausible explanations come to mind. The union driver for a large firm operates within a highly structured system. The truck he drives will be turned over to another driver at a fixed terminal, and violations of speed limits will accomplish very little. The independent, conversely, is likely to drive the same truck from point of origin to destination, and whatever time he spends resting will result only in later delivery of his cargo. With a huge number of independents on the road, safety inspectors cannot locate them all, let alone subject them to rigorous enforcement of safety standards. A strong union, by the same token, contributes to safety by making it difficult for firms to pressure drivers into violating safety rules.

In mid-1979, a reporter rode with an independent automobile hauler, whose usual route began near Pittsburgh, where he lived. He went first to Detroit to pick up cars, then to the docks in New Jersey, and then home. In one three-year period of his 17-year driving career, he had driven the 580-mile round trip from Pittsburgh to Detroit and back every day, seven days a week, something he could not do without violating time limits. He admitted to the reporter that he usually drove at 65-to-70 miles per hour ("engine efficiency"), and, when the reporter noticed stay-awake pills in the truck, the driver said that while he would not be above taking them, he generally did not.[25] Many suspect that amphetamine use is widespread among unregulated drivers, because they could not otherwise sustain the long driving periods that enable them to compete.

With the reform of 1980, thousands of new firms entered the industry; many individuals mortgaged themselves to the hilt to buy second-hand rigs, each confident that lots of business awaited him. When, early in 1983, new legislation enacted higher user fees, violence again returned to the highways. While it is easy to condemn truckers for resorting to violence, the critics should acknowledge that when people find themselves in desperate situations, their reactions are unpredictable. Few advocates of deregulation, moreover, notice that the contemporary trend toward supertrucks, or "warehouses on wheels" — a trend which threatens to damage highways and increase traffic deaths — is wholly traceable to deregulation. Locked in desperate price wars, companies feel they must use giant trucks to cut costs. Tragically, believers in the free market are content to have the accident problem solved through the loss of insurance coverage for those having accidents, a solution that does not help the dead.

Like the CAB, the ICC took on its regulatory function when there already were too many companies and trucks, and, also like the CAB, it could not limit schedule frequency. The regulated trucking industry, then, was indeed inefficient, but the waste was traceable to competition, not regulation. In such industries, the right of an individual to buy a truck and start a business must be limited. The truckers now falling by the economic wayside in large numbers are not casualties of their own mismanagement, but are victims of misguided policy. As in so many other industries, the waste represented by trucks left to rust, because their owners are in bankruptcy, exceeds anything government could waste if it tried.

The trucking industry is not unique in this respect, but it typifies how economic theology overlooks related questions. Whatever any reader may think of the feasibility of a national civil-defense effort to protect citizens from the possible outcomes of nuclear war, trucking could be important to any such effort. If citizens are to evacuate major cities and take up temporary residence in rural areas, how might they be expected to survive without regular shipment of food and other supplies? Ironically, the interstate highway system was justified in part by national defense needs, and military vehicles are not the only ones of any significance. A full-fledged trucking system would include a number of cargo terminals for freight transshipment, driver rest and replacement, maintenance, and refueling. In a well-managed system, terminals would not be located on the basis of a single company's operations, but would be located on the basis of areawide needs. Regional regulatory bodies could determine the amount of service needed for small communities (and their small businesses), and might also be involved in civil-defense planning.

The immediate future is not promising, but the absence of data will prevent intelligent discussion. There is likely to be periodic violence, and new forms of antitrust collusion among shippers. Groups of medium-sized shippers probably will secretly band together and seek low rates from weaker truckers.[26] Other problems doubtless will resemble those now emerging in the more visible bus industry. Meanwhile, we are left to wonder why Ris, a prominent congressional staff member, would pronounce a rise in the number of bankruptcies as a sign of success. Economic theology, unfortunately, breeds callousness.

BUSES: STRANDING SMALL-TOWN AMERICA

The bus industry became, late in 1982, only the latest of the transportation industries to be thrown open to unbridled competition. The results thus far have been poignant. For many years, small communities located along deserted railroad tracks have depended upon the buses, but it now appears that small-town America is being cut off from the outside world.

It took Greyhound very little time to decide that in a deregulated environment, it should abandon 1,313 communities in 43 states. With profits declining, and with competition threatening to become more intense on major routes, the company's decision was understandable. As rural and semirural Americans now find themselves increasingly isolated, except for those who own, and are able to drive, automobiles, the effects of deregulation of trucks and of buses come together in obscene ways. In Gonzales, Texas, for example, three auto-parts stores and the only hospital in town made it known that they were dependent upon Greyhound's package service for everything from spark plugs to blood units.[27]

Other stories are similarly distressing. The city administrator of Tiffin, Ohio, a town of 20,000 located 60 miles from Toledo, commented on the loss of bus service:

> We understand that from an economic standpoint. But we have people who are not being served and we know, particularly, the abandonment has created hardship for elderly people.

Joyce Bailes, whose family had operated a Greyhound agency in Herrin, Illinois, since 1934, noted that while businessmen might be able to drive ten miles to pick up packages delivered to the next town, low-income travelers "can't afford to pay a cab to go ten miles to catch a bus." Ethia Perliman, a 72-year-old resident of Unadilla, New York, asserted that she "really shouldn't drive those distances alone" (to Oneonta and Albany to see a physician and shop). Pat Vogel, the Greyhound station manager in Sidney, New York, claimed that the company was not losing money in serving 14 small towns between Albany and Binghamton:

> What I collect for tickets is classified, but I can tell you it runs to four figures every month and I know for sure Greyhound isn't losing money.[28]

At a time when government at last has paid some attention to the needs of handicapped people, the last connection between much of rural America and the outside world has been broken.

The deregulators, of course, may be correct. Perhaps some enterprising trucker will offer to move very small packages in very small vehicles to and from Gonzales and the eight other towns between Houston and San Antonio that Greyhound has abandoned. Yet those who have foisted deregulation upon us hardly took time to notice that for many towns, Greyhound served as a mover of both people and freight. Deregulation, by making it impossible to collect data, will, once again, make it almost impossible to produce evidence that there is a problem at all. Other results of bus deregulation are even more arcane.

The California Public Utilities Commission decided in 1981 that even though it had regulated tour buses since 1927, it really had no legal authority to do so. Hoping that all-out competition would lead to better quality and lower prices, the commission turned loose the tour-bus industry — whereupon prices steeply rose. For those interested in visiting Beverly Hills, Universal Studios, Disneyland, and Yosemite, prices jumped 15-to-20 percent following deregulation, and the story is fascinating. Many new companies entered the business but, since they found themselves competing for the same tourists, all companies now have many more empty seats than the old companies used to have. The competition immediately became stiff; where two regulated firms once operated in Anaheim, five unregulated ones now compete.

Anaheim is not unique. The Gray Line operator in Los Angeles lost hundreds of thousands of dollars in 1982, the first loss in more than a decade. Even with 12.4 million visitors to the city, an increase from 1981, the company averaged ten more empty seats per trip than before. After many years in which it had raised prices by 1 or 2 percent per year, Gray Line prices recently were 50 percent higher than they had been only three years earlier. What happened?

Tourists are almost captive passengers. Arriving in a strange city, they feel they cannot afford to spend much time in comparison shopping. They turn instead to a hotel bell captain, and thereby hangs a tale. The captains once gathered commissions of 10-to-15 percent for recruiting passengers, but they now can get 20 percent by auctioning themselves to competing bus operators. Some of the captains have become more entrepreneurial; in peak periods, they join forces to charter their own tour buses, grossing up to $1,000 per day after paying only $200 for the charter.[29] Is it possible that California may find it necessary to regulate the bell captains?

Meanwhile, the situation should be familiar to anyone who stops to think about how transportation systems must function. Obviously, a 150-percent increase in the number of bus companies in Anaheim (and a 400-percent increase in San Francisco) could lead to lower prices only if the number of tourists increased even more. Yet this would have required a sudden and huge increase in hotel rooms and tourist attractions. If the tourists now must pay for all the empty seats in the buses they ride, the fares are high enough to allow top-quality maintenance. This is not the case everywhere.

The American Bus Association conducts annually a travel bazaar; tour-bus and resort operators come together for a week to make their deals for the upcoming year. Literally hundreds of tables are set up in giant halls, and there are so many buyers and sellers that each participant is limited to a single brief period at a table in the morning, and another in the afternoon. When the bell rings, advertisements come down while others go up. In visiting the 1983 gathering, I spoke with a number of bus operators from Florida, where intrastate buses have been deregulated for a few years. Stories are not scientific evidence but, as in trucking, nothing else will be available unless regulation is reinstated.

Confident they could make a go of it, some bus drivers quit their companies, bought their own second-hand buses, and began their own charter businesses. Forced to cut costs to the bone in order to attract riders, they began to neglect necessary maintenance. Without mechanics or facilities of their own, they now must take their buses to garages. Experienced garage operators told me that in a number of instances, they had worked on buses having only one or two brakes in working order. Floridians may be lucky; the state does not have hills. But the state government cannot be expected to hire enough inspectors to keep up with every small operator, and disasters beckon.

If the transportation industries are now being reduced to shambles due to the banner of free-market theology, it is worth recalling again that competition wrecked the railroads long ago, and not only in the nineteenth century. Unregulated growth and ineffectively regulated competition led to chaos, whatever analysts might prefer to ascribe to corporate greed and mismanagement. Veteran travelers may recall when Chicago had about a half-dozen railroad stations, in different parts of the city, that made connections very difficult. Longtime railroad watchers may remember the dream of one railroad president, Robert Young of the New York Central, who wanted to bring the railroads into the twentieth century. His slogan, in the 1940s, was: "A pig can travel in a single railroad car from coast to coast, but you cannot."

If the country's transportation systems are ever to make sense, tough choices lie ahead. Economists notwithstanding, transportation systems have largely identical characteristics. The fact that five airlines or truck companies can dispatch vehicles on the same route at the same time, using public airways and highways, does not mean this should be allowed to happen. With reluctance, some economists do admit that because of the high fixed costs of building a railroad, it can be considered a "natural monopoly," but one cannot be sure.

It is possible even now that U.S. development of "bullet-trains," the high-speed operations now in France and Japan, will fall prey to classical economics. After all, someone may produce calculations showing that there should be, say, three competing bullet-trains operating between New York and Washington on parallel tracks. If this argument seems unlikely to surface, I can offer a relevant personal experience. I once mentioned to a Department of Transportation economist that municipal bus service was one transportation example not logically eligible for a free-market approach. His response, startling at the time, was that bus service would indeed be improved by direct competition. In retrospect, I should not have been startled at all.

Only minimal optimism is in order, even though planning for the first American bullet-train has begun. The California legislature recently approved $1.25 billion in tax-exempt bonds to finance a 160-mile-per-hour train between Los Angeles and San Diego. The American High Speed Rail Corporation plans to make a test run of it by 1985, and to be in full operation (50 daily round trips) by 1988. The company, whose president doubles as an Amtrak executive, was formed because Amtrak knew it could get no federal funds for the project, and because private investors would not put money into a project controlled by a quasi-governmental organization such as Amtrak. It is somehow typical that the United States, borrowing in this case from French and Japanese government-developed-and-operated systems, would insist upon a private-enterprise approach.[30] Assuming the line is built as planned, Los Angeles-San Diego travelers will be able to drive, ride the train, choose from the four airlines now serving the route, or choose from among several bus companies. For nondrivers in small towns along the way, travel may be wholly impossible. Small wonder that American transportation policies are the world's laughingstock.

The new plight of small-town America is directly connected with the fallacies of economic theory. A major philosophical premise of economics is the ability of the free market to meet the needs of the individual. This sometimes is described as the market's response to individual differences in style, taste, and quality. Yet unless large groups of individuals have identical preferences, no producer will respond to those desires. The result is that, if very large numbers of people travel between major cities, they will have many more alternatives than they need. Those stranded in small towns, of course, cannot find anyone to serve them. So much for the claims of theology. Only a form of regulation can serve the individual.

THE SHIPS ARE NOT AT SEA

While not a subject of recent major policy decisions across the board, the shipping industry remains an obvious example of why regulation ultimately must become global. As one report put it early in 1983, "The world's major harbors are jammed with vessels built to transport American grain to the Soviet Union, Saudi oil to France, Japanese video recorders to Britain." At the end of 1982, 15 million deadweight tons worth of dry-bulk carriers were laid up (almost four times as much as in 1979), along with 90 million tons worth of tankers (triple 1979 figures).[31]

Observers are likely to blame the overcapacity on world economic conditions, ignoring the possibility that when "too many ships are chasing too few customers" (as one report noted), the problem is just that: too many ships. The world's maritime fleets have been trapped for many years in the depression sequence but, since ocean vessels are seldom noticed by most citizens, the sequence gets little attention. As rates plummet in global price wars (many rates are only half what they were in 1981), operators seek cheaper labor and skimp on training, thereby increasing safety risks. Occasional strikes (mutinies) are reported, as crews rebel. About $20 billion in bank loans stands at risk around the world ($10-$15 billion in this country) and, if loans guaranteed by governments are included, perhaps $100 billion is endangered.

Meanwhile, American coastal ports must vigorously compete against each other for present and future cargoes. Philadelphia recently launched a $1-million marketing campaign, succeeding in diverting Chilean fruit shipments from New York. The latter retaliated by developing a package that lured cocoa beans from Philadelphia. Union concessions and other give-backs were involved.[32]

The Reagan administration, admitting that American ports would have to be expanded to accommodate huge coal carriers, asserted that if the Army Engineers were to widen and deepen channels to the required 60-foot depths (European ports had begun doing this), "user fees" would have to pay the bills.[33]

It may be the case that complete channel access to all of the old major ports — a responsibility of federal government — no longer makes economic sense. Depending upon what any observer believes to be the future of war, channel dredging might become a defense requirement. In the competitive struggle among the ports, however, "user fees" will inevitably be extracted from dock workers in the form of poverty wages, and from consumers.* While these questions intersect with other issues to be outlined later, the pattern here is clear: New outbreaks of waterfront violence are likely as the struggle for survival continues.

ATTENTION, SPORTS FANS

Professional sports appear to be activities outside the normal boundaries of serious analysis, given the image of the blue-collar worker who sits in front of a television set while guzzling beer. Yet professional sports have much to tell us about issues of regulation and deregulation because, taken together, recent labor troubles in baseball, football, and basketball highlight virtually all the related economic questions.

The baseball major leagues have had, for more than a half-century, a grant of antitrust immunity but, in recent years, owner-player relationships have undergone a significant change. After long and expensive litigation, big-league players finally secured a limited right to free agency. After playing for a specified number of years, a player is no longer bound to a team for his career, but can offer his services to the highest bidder. George Steinbrenner, the shipping tycoon who owns the New York Yankees, and Gene Autry, the former singing cowboy who owns the California Angels, have

---

*Note that, as in the case of user fees for Coast Guard emergency assistance, this could even transform items of national defense from public goods (paid for by all citizens) to private goods supported by those having any transactions with parts of the defense establishment. Might the citizen one day have to pay the cost of the police investigation of a burglary at her home?

been among the leaders in luring superstars with lucrative contracts, and other teams have followed. The $1-million salary for playing ball has become common. Marvin Miller, retired director of the players' union, has been hailed as one of the most successful of unionists, for even marginal (utility) players have been paid $400,000 annual salaries.

Bidding wars led to huge increases in payrolls – a problem in this sport because the major leagues financially support their own farm systems for training young players. For quite a while, few believed the baseball owners when they asserted that the high payrolls might destroy the sport. Gradually, however, it became clearer that payrolls could not escalate forever; and, seeking to change what they regarded as a runaway system, the owners went on strike in 1981 – an action widely misunderstood.

When it was time to renegotiate the labor contract in 1981, the players had no substantial demands to make. The owners insisted that players "give back" some of the rights won in court. After a long unpaid vacation, the players gave in. They agreed that any team losing a free agent would be compensated by choosing another player from a replacement pool designated for that purpose. As of mid-1983, this change had not appreciably slowed down bidding wars, the effects of which remained largely unnoticed. Put simply, the costs of the wars were being transferred to taxpayers and consumers.

According to contract arrangements made when a municipal stadium opened in Pittsburgh in 1970, for example, the Pirates were to maintain the stadium. Claiming that low attendance and high payrolls made this impossible, the Pirates implied that unless the contract were renegotiated, they might move to another city. The mayor then concluded a pact with the team's owners, agreeing that the city would repair and maintain the stadium. Local corporations, among them a floundering U.S. Steel Corporation, chipped in more than $12 million for repairs, in return for having advertising displayed in the stadium. Affluent citizens were persuaded to lease new luxury boxes, most of them tax deductible. Meanwhile, the Pirates were following what had become a typical pattern: In order to keep even marginal players, contracts must be guaranteed, but, in some cases, the players' performances became so unsatisfactory that they must be released – and paid not to play.

New York City spent more than $100 million to refurbish Yankee·Stadium, thereby releasing funds for Steinbrenner to use in bidding wars. The Philadelphia Phillies, among the most successful of teams in luring customers, announced that they were losing money because of a very large number of very high-salaried players. The Montreal Expos, successful ticket sellers also, announced they could no longer afford to pay the rent demanded by the city, and negotiated to play their games in Vancouver; but the Montreal government relented just before the 1983 season began. All across the country, cities are using tax breaks and other subsidies, in part to encourage teams to stay where they are, but, in large measure, to compensate for price wars. Baseball deregulation conforms in many ways to free-market theology, but how long can it be sustained?

The drama in football has followed a somewhat different, but an equally interesting script. The National Football League (NFL) achieved success through revenue sharing, often labeled "NFL socialism." The huge income from network television was divided equally among all teams, enabling them all to pay high-enough salaries to star rookies who might otherwise have played in Canada. While the players had the right to move from team to team, no football team attempted to acquire even one of the superstar free agents. Concluding that because teams received the same income for winning or losing, the owners were left with no incentive to bid, the players put forth what was thought, in 1982, to be a novel proposal.

The players struck when owners rejected their demand to extend "NFL socialism" to include the players. The proposal was to use slightly more than half of total revenues for a salary pool, to be distributed according to scales that had yet to be negotiated. While a majority of low-salaried players supported the strike, some of the higher-paid stars did not. The owners denounced the proposal as an "un-American" attempt to make players the "partners" of management. Ultimately, the players surrendered. Meanwhile, continued success in marketing professional football encouraged the formation of yet another new league (the United States Football League), and the planning for still a third (the International Football League), promising only that multileague bidding wars might escalate.

The future of professional-sports self-regulation may have been established by the mid-1983 agreement of basketball owners and players. The commissioner of the National Basketball Association (NBA), Lawrence O'Brien, is a former postmaster general and was a close political associate of John F. Kennedy. As the most politically astute of sports commissioners, he can be assumed to have a sophisticated view of how to go about gaining antitrust immunity for professional sports.* Acting as his own chief negotiator, O'Brien successfully pressured the owners to make the very same proposal made only a few months earlier by football players. Despite substantial television income and fairly good attendance figures, bidding wars for basketball players had soared to unbelievable heights, some players commanding $2-million annual salaries. Even with tax breaks from some cities owning municipal arenas, many of the teams were in serious financial trouble. When the players agreed to the proposal, a new age may have dawned.

By the mid-1980s, basketball players' salaries will be tied to revenues, and these will be adjusted if cable revenues become significant; effectively, player salaries have been capped, and will rise or fall with income. As the owners and players signed their new contract, they smilingly addressed each other as "partners," realizing they had joined in a regulatory scheme that some would label socialism. To be sure, consumers will be involved, for all of us contribute to advertising payments and, in turn, to the salaries paid to Frank Gifford and Howard Cosell for bringing us prime-time football. Runaway bidding wars must now come to a halt, at least in basketball. O'Brien doubtless believes the agreement will survive an antitrust challenge because the workers have accepted his scheme.

The basketball agreement is indeed wide-ranging. For those teams having the lowest cash flows and payrolls, the entire league will subsidize salaries to the level of agreed floors (90 percent of the ceilings). The purpose is to prevent a team in a large market (New York) from destroying competitive balance. While this will be easier to manage for small basketball squads than for larger teams in other

---

*Sports illustrate some of the antitrust fallacies. A league cannot schedule games or matches unless there is collusion among allegedly private firms. However, one recent court decision held that the NFL could not prevent one of its owners from moving his team to any city he chose. If the decision were to stand, the indemnity payments would be costly to the league.

sports, the idea is sound. Veteran sports observers, including a law professor who studies sports law, know that more people buy tickets when competition is keen.[34] To reach an agreement, players and owners abandoned free-market principles, and the latter, with only an occasional protest, opened their financial records to players — an unusual action in an industry long marked by team secrecy.

Assuming this form of regulation works as well as seems likely, the next step should be for municipal-arena owners to reexamine the tax breaks already granted to teams, often for the sake of bribing them to stay. All-out competition among states and cities for sports teams, and the building of convention centers, and of new industries as well, clearly have gotten out of hand. With less than enough large conventions to fully occupy all convention centers, for example, cities must outbid each other in price wars that taxpayers ultimately subsidize. Any system of sensible regulation, then, immediately suggests wider application of its principles.

As in so many other sectors, it is unfortuate that those involved in professional sports seldom understand the absurdities of economic thought and of antitrust law. Few people inside and outside sports commented on the oddity of having owners and players in one sport take positions precisely the opposite of those of their contemporaries in another sport. One of the top player agents, who agreed before the settlement that the basketball league was in poor financial shape, blamed the "avarice and greed of the owners who submitted to all these large salaries."[35] He apparently forgot that huge losses are not evidence of greed, but, rather, evidence that in all-out competition, the competitors simply must compete. Meanwhile, the baseball owners continue to follow their tradition of secrecy. They quietly adopted in 1982 a rule that each team could have no less than a ratio of 60-40 with respect to assets and liabilities. When this became known some months later, the players' union filed a grievance on grounds that this was an illegal conspiracy to limit player salaries.[36] When might the basketball regulatory framework become a model instead of an exception?

MONEY AT LARGE, BANKS IN CRISIS

If Milton and Rose Friedman are correct, the Great Depression began on December 11, 1930, when the Bank of the United States, in New York, closed its doors. While there earlier had been small runs on banks in the Midwest and the South, the New York bank was the largest single failure in American history. According to the Friedmans, the Federal Reserve and other banks should have joined forces to prevent the closing, but myopic policy making and even anti-Semitism caused them to do nothing (the bank served largely Jewish customers).[37] Today, one reads every day that the world banking system faces a "crisis"; that U.S. banks have many outstanding loans that may never be repaid; that the world's monetary "system" is in shambles; and, indeed, that large banks are failing from time to time.

Many remain puzzled that even with rising unemployment and falling prices, interest rates remained very high in 1983. The standard explanations were that the Federal Reserve Board had been too restrictive with the total supply of money; that (conversely) it had been "too loose"; that government deficit spending had driven up the cost of money to other borrowers; that the money supply was too "volatile"; and that the all-purpose alibi of economics (psychological expectations) had again arisen. While Milton Friedman admitted that "nobody really understands what's going on," a handful of observers noted that the problem might be the deregulation of the financial industry.[38] Yet the real problem may be easier to understand than are the problems economists invent because they cannot see what has happened. While the process is not yet complete, banks are being permitted to move across state boundaries and, in some cases, to compete nationally for borrowers and depositors. They also have been turned loose to offer any interest rates they choose.

As banks offer higher rates to depositors, competing banks must do the same thing, but what must banks do next? If they are to make profits, the banks must lend money at rates higher than they pay depositors. This encourages risky and speculative loans, and many such loans have been made. Similarly, they must set higher rates for citizens who sign up for automobiles, appliances, and homes, thereby discouraging a recovery in those industries. Since the depositors tend to be richer and older than the borrowers, the result is a "reverse-transfer payment" from the younger middle class to the older rich,[39] but that is not the only dubious outcome.

Martin Mayer notes that the combination of interest-rate wars and depositor insurance has led to a "nutty" result. Because the

Federal Deposit Insurance Corporation and the Federal Savings and Loan Insurance Corporation insure the principal and interest on deposits, bankers know that the government guarantees payment even if banks earn far less with the money. Suggesting that deposit insurance should be restricted to the principal alone, Mayer adds that the 1983 decision to permit accounts with unlimited interest and unlimited checks must soon lead to the end of free checking. This situation exists because Congress responded so quickly to the need of bankers for a "product" to compete with money-market funds.[40]

Interest-rate competition encouraged citizens to increase savings so that investors would then step up the building of new plants and the purchase of new equipment. With the world banking industry teetering because loans for expansion may never be repaid, there is some hesitancy on the part of lenders to continue overbuilding, even if the dominant solution is to lend more to borrowers who show no signs of being able to repay. Tax-deferring retirement accounts and interest-rate wars lured new savings, but these seemed to go into inflating stocks. In everyday economic jargon, buying stocks is considered "investment" but, in the truest sense of the word, there is no investment unless the capital goes into new plants. The indications in mid-1983 were that savings were being plowed into stock speculation, and that a bank-market crash was possible.[41]

All-out competition among banks, money markets, and savings and loans associations has produced a confusing environment in which potential depositors are buffeted by questionable advertising. In one case, a major New York bank advertised in bold type that interest paid on its new money-market deposit accounts was 10.5 percent for balances up to $15,000 and 11 percent for higher balances, but only in tiny print below was it mentioned that the rates were guaranteed only until the following Monday.[42] This was followed by the counteradvertising of money-market mutual funds, which warned that banks might not give depositors a fair share of the profits made from bank money-market accounts, but added that the mutual funds were required by law to distribute all the income earned by the funds.[43]

If the theory argued in this book is correct, the slowdown in new investment occurred because global plant capacity was already overbuilt. Public and private banks had competed for years in trying to outdo each other in lending both in this country and abroad.

Susan Kaufman Purcell, of the Council on Foreign Relations, outlined how this worked with respect to Mexico:

> Assuming that oil prices would continue rising, Mexico adopted an ambitious development strategy involving large-scale Government spending of petroleum-generated revenues to modernize industry, stimulate private investment and reduce unemployment. The ensuing inflation was to be offset by increases in productivity. But . . . world oil prices and consumption declined, interest rates increased and the world's industrial economies entered into a recession. . . .
>
> . . . foreign banks repeatedly raised lending limits. Why not? As Mexico's . . . situation deteriorated, the cost of loans increased. Bank profits soared, as did the temptation to lend more money; . . . banks competed with one another; as long as some would lend, those refusing to do so risked exclusion from the Mexican market once the situation improved. . . . United States banks — creditors for between $18 billion and $34 billion — apparently convinced themselves that Mexico knew what it was doing — and that if Mexico did not, Washington would bail it out.[44]

The voices raised in protest against interest-rate bidding wars were relatively few in number, and their arguments were not wholly consistent with each other, but they were the voices of careful analysts who had the qualifications to issue warnings. To the average borrower, the banks have become "loan sharks," and to the big speculators in foreign investments and the stock market, "the door of the vault gapes as wide as the loan officer's smile.[45] Because this depression is the first one to mix an economic slump with high interest rates, deregulation may be the primary cause of the problem. The competition among the banks compelled each bank to keep its loan portfolios at least as high as those of its major competitors, but, since economic theology holds that overexpansion generally is impossible, every individual decision was defensible on that basis. Following the collapse of a bank in Oklahoma (the fourth largest failure in American history), but just before a still larger collapse in Tennessee, one economic analyst summarized the situation as follows:

> . . . there is a time bomb ticking away in financial markets; many of the "assets" listed on the plus side of commercial banks' assets sheets are worthless loans; . . . you can bet more will surface before we get out of this mess.[46]

While interest-rate deregulation made it impossible for interest rates to decline, the larger problem is traceable to the sudden increases in oil prices that began in 1973. The members of the Organization of Petroleum Exporting Countries (OPEC) found themselves awash in capital, much of which they deposited in Western banks (i.e., recycling). The banks, with few investment opportunities at home, lent billions and billions to developing countries and to planned economies in the Eastern bloc. By mid-1982, American banks alone had $69.7 billion outstanding in Latin America, $27.7 billion in Asia, $4.5 billion in Africa, $23.1 billion in OPEC countries, $6.4 billion in the Eastern bloc, and $14.6 billion in offshore banking centers.[47] The "problem loans" of the World Bank had jumped from the normal 8-to-9 percent to 12 percent.[48]

If investment opportunities within the United States amount to less than the money available to invest, this is a signal that global industrial capacity is already exceeding demand. Yet it is clear that the money lent to overseas borrowers is to go into new plant capacity that exceeds the domestic needs of the borrowers, as in the case of the $9.2 billion lent to South Korea by American banks. Logically, the new plants will seek to sell their output to the customers now buying from older plants in the United States and elsewhere. If the new plants succeed, industries in advanced countries will suffer, and the banks with them. If the new plants fail, the banks also suffer. Thus, each bank competes against itself — truly a no-win game.

When the follies of the late 1970s were combined with the interest-rate wars of the early 1980s, the result was a headlong rush to disaster. Reregulation of interest rates would be a modest first step on the road to sanity, but even this could not by itself solve the global banking crisis. While extended analysis is beyond the scope of this effort, solutions cannot merely involve manipulation of the money supply, whether in the monetarist or the Keynesian mode. All attempts to solve economic problems through increases or decreases in money stock incorrectly assume that the problems lie more in money management than in the production and distribution systems the money supply supports. Thus, interest-rate deregulation merely made a bad situation quickly worse. On this, a post-Keynesian perspective may be useful.[49]

It remains to be seen if the historic antitrust pattern will assert itself in the financial industry. If large firms, banks in this instance, ultimately compete coast-to-coast, they could, in principle, outbid competing banks by offering very high interest rates to depositors. The other banks, by definition, must meet the competition and, in so doing, would collapse. If and when failures occur, however, will those left standing be accused of having engaged in "predatory pricing" for the sake of driving competitors out of business? The question implies that the same type of analysis is applicable to any industry. In the classical mythology, a large firm lowers prices until it drives competitors to ruin, then raises them when it has something close to monopoly power. In the reverse form of competition in which banks (and professional-sports owners) engage, a firm might raise offers until competitors drop out. Using an argument first advanced by John S. McGee, Dominick Armentano shows that, at least in principle, the concept of predatory pricing has little merit:

> . . . such practices are very costly for the large firm; it always stands relatively more to lose since it, by definition, does the most business. . . . The uncertainty of the length of the forthcoming battle, and thus its indeterminate expense, must surely make firms wary of initiating a price war. . . . Competitors can simply close down and wait for the price to return to profitable levels; or new owners might purchase bankrupt facilities and ready them to compete with the predator. . . . Such wars inevitably spread to surrounding markets, endangering the predator's profits in his "safe" areas. And . . . predatory practices . . . already assume a "war chest" of monopoly profits to see the firm through the costly battles; firms apparently cannot initiate predatory practices unless they already possess monopoly power. But if this is true, firms cannot gain initial monopoly positions through predatory practices.[50]

The conclusion appears valid for banks. To drive competitors out of business, a large bank would offer predatorily high interest rates, but it would then have to seek borrowers able and willing to pay loan-shark interest rates on loans. Those borrowing at such rates would default in large numbers, bringing the predatory banker to his knees. The larger point is that in classical price competition, prices fall until entire industries collapse. In the reverse price competition outlined here, high interest rates must inevitably lead to widespread defaults. The large firms, then, become the target of antitrust action, and reverse predatory pricing the crime.

If one follows the reports of the global banking crisis, many loans never will be repaid. Alfred Gailord Hart, professor emeritus of economics at Columbia, concludes that "any orderly solution [to the international debt problem] must entail writing off enough of the debt to leave a tenable structure." He is willing to accept a "giveaway program" so that victims of crop failures will not starve, but not willing "to arm Argentina against Chile and Chile against Argentina."[51] The global financial crisis, then, is traceable to the same factors that caused the depression of the 1890s (as outlined in Chapter 1). If many of the loans ultimately must be forgiven, the "giveaways" would have been put to much better use had they been assigned to the building of roads, bridges, water systems, and other items of social infrastructure. Following the classical theology, however, banks (correctly, in their view) lend money for projects that, according to theology, will ultimately pay for themselves, but will not lend money for public works that, in principle, will not pay for themselves in hard cash.

By mid-1983, some progress was being made in refinancing, rolling over, or otherwise making it possible for some countries to at least keep up the interest payments on their loans. While this was being defined as a "solution," important factors were being underpublicized. The banks involved in refinancing were collecting substantial fees that made them appear profitable and enabled them to continue carrying loans on their books as "collectable," even though the collateral, or security, for the loans was industrial plants almost bound not to succeed. A prominent British banker acknowledged that banks had for years "been doing things that well-brought-up bankers never did, that is to say, lending money in situations when they knew they had no hope of getting it back." His solution was to shift some uncollectable loans to central banks or to the International Monetary Fund, which, in turn, would sell bonds and pay off the banks who cannot now collect. Any such improvements could be only illusory. (On how double-entry bookkeeping fosters such illusions, see Chapter 6.) Ultimately, these loans will become giveaways that could offer a better economic stimulus if they had been used for public works in the first place.[52]

If and when this financial mess is recognized, giveaway agreements should not be limited to foreign borrowers. Many people in this country, whose unemployment or underemployment is traceable to the American fascination with free markets, and who cannot meet the high loan payments levied upon them, will need forgiveness if they are not to be ruined for life. Among such people are, for example, those who believed their leaders and rushed to sign up for trucks, only to find there was no business for them. Charles Peters, drawing upon the experience of the Great Depression, recently suggested that if deposit insurance helped save the banks in the 1930s, "consumer insurance" might help now. His aim was to encourage employed people to go out and buy now; government would tax them later if they fell behind on loan payments. If they lost their jobs, however, the government would pay off the loans.[53] The larger implications are treated in the final chapter.

ARE TELEPHONES PUBLIC UTILITIES?

Hardly anyone argued that AT & T was not a reasonably innovative and efficient organization. John Kenneth Galbraith, a prominent contemporary liberal (some might label him a "closet socialist") who acknowledges the need for large organizations, has praised the American communications system and the firm responsible for it. Urban and interurban surface transportation suffered, by comparison. In retrospect, the latter

> required that there be one corporation, that is to say, one planning instrument, covering the cities of an entire region including the lines between. The local systems would then have been developed in relation to the intercity and interregional system with joint use of rights-of-way, terminals and other facilities as appropriate. The prospective growth of the entire system would have been projected in a systematic and orderly way together with the investment requirements in the various parts and at various stages. A planning unit of such scope and power would have been largely independent of local influences and pressures in setting fares. Prices, in other words, would have been wholly or largely under its planning control.[54]

Galbraith outlined what might have occurred if the communications system had developed in the same manner as did transportation:

> Had local telephone service been provided by one or more companies in each city, town or hamlet; had all these rates been subject to local regulation and influence; had long-distance service been provided by numerous separate companies, only loosely coordinated with local service; had there been little or no research and technical development

anywhere in the system; had the local units been strongly dependent on external authority — municipal government or local banks — for capital; and had there been no planned provision for labor supply or substitute technology, it seems unlikely that telephone communications could have survived in any very useful form.[55]

Galbraith could not have foreseen in the 1960s, when he wrote those words, that his hypothetical look back would become a prophecy of what likely will happen between now and the end of the century. The national communications system may turn out to be the greatest casualty ever in regard to an American commitment to economic theology. It has been destroyed solely because it did not conform to the ideal of competition: so long as competition is possible, it should be not only permitted, but required. That view has now prevailed.

A scheme of regulation must be organizationally appropriate to the industry being regulated. The regulatory framework for overseeing "Ma Bell" fell short. The long-distance telephone service was regulated by the Federal Communications Commission (FCC), while state commissions supervised local subdivisions. Not only was there a disastrous lack of coordination among these regulatory systems, but the activism of local antimonopoly groups had the effect of pressuring AT & T into keeping local service rates as low as possible. The real price of local service declined substantially over the years; telephones became an integral part of the lifestyle of many citizens who, before World War II, could not afford them. With urban areas constantly expanding, and with even local travel often becoming more difficult, the telephone became a lifeline, especially for the poor, the ill, and the handicapped. This is the issue which ultimately must be faced. In the absence of an articulated public policy, AT & T operated a hidden social-welfare system. The revenues from long-distance service, much of them derived from business, supported local systems, including services that cannot be left to market decisions. Pay telephones on street corners are expensive to install and maintain; yet they may be necessary as matters of public interest. The same can be said for pay telephones in all sorts of locations, from drugstores to theaters and transportation terminals. For obvious reasons, such pay stations must be connected to the long-distance systems if they are to exist at all. It was the costs of long-distance service that broke the back of the Bell System.

When it became obvious that satellite, microwave, and cable technologies would make possible the development of new long-distance systems, the FCC decided that long-distance should be thrown open to free-market competition. When this compelled AT & T to reduce its long-distance rates in order to stay abreast of its competitors, local regulatory agencies and interest groups mistakenly concluded that they were being subjected to the typically high-handed practices of monopoly. This spurred the bandwagon organized to "break up Bell," and few voices were raised in opposition. After the Bell System becomes dismantled, as of January 1, 1984, 22 subsidiaries will organize into seven regional companies. Various state regulators and consumer-interest groups challenged the divestiture plan in 1983, arguing, in effect, that AT & T was "dumping" obsolete equipment on local companies while taking for itself some more modern facilities (charge-a-call phones, for example).[56] It is conceivable that arrangements more favorable to local companies might have been worked out, but those opposing the terms of divestiture were only then coming to realize that deregulation would leave them with the toughest political problem of all. Having incorrectly assumed that the free market would lower prices everywhere (isn't that what the textbooks say?), they were looking for ways out of a trap they had closed around themselves.

As of mid-1983, some of the more specific predictions not only threatened the typical local telephone users — those in urban areas — but bode something close to disaster for many others. The Florida Public Service Commission announced that within a year, the average residential rate for Southern Bell users would jump from $10.65 to $31.15. A financial officer of New York Telephone said it would need $2.9 million in new revenues by the end of 1985, an amount greater than all the rate increases of the past 13 years. This might increase the average consumer's bill by 50-to-70 percent in two years, and others predicted a doubling or tripling of rates within five years. Indeed, Southwestern Bell submitted in mid-1983 a request for a $1.7 billion rate increase, one that immediately would triple (from $10 to $30) the average monthly bill for 4.5 million customers in Texas, predicting that the average would rise to $50 within five years.[57] Few people understood that despite the dominance of AT & T, small, independent phone companies had operated for many years. According to the president of the Pennsylvania Independent Telephone Association, these companies long had a "basic, clearly defined, longstanding method of dividing toll revenues with the Bell System" — an arrangement now coming to an end. Eventually, those in rural areas may have to pay the full costs of stringing access lines to their homes. As one independent operator in Pennsylvania put it:

> Can you imagine the guy who builds out in the boonies — how much he'll have to pay to have telephone lines constructed? It could be $5,000.[58]

Like those now to be stranded without bus service, these rural Americans have relatively little political clout.

Meanwhile, few believed AT & T when it predicted early in 1982 that in five years, its share of the long-distance market would drop below 50 percent. By October, however, it was clear that its prediction was not far off, and that long-distance competition resembled the California tour-bus business. Small entrepreneurs, unable to build their own complete networks, had launched a new industry labeled "reselling." They bought WATS lines from AT & T, entitling them to cheap long-distance service, and then sold time on those lines to several customers, much as bell captains chartered buses in Anaheim.

Resellers are not always small businesses. Satelco, not the largest such firm, decided to make a public stock offering in mid-1983. Its two owners, a former restauranteur and his father-in-law, could wind up with about $70 million in stock and $1 million in cash. From a larger perspective, these new wholesalers, or middle-men, siphon off funds once used to cross-subsidize local services. When a larger system is torn asunder in this manner, questions of equity are overlooked.[59]

Among others, Peter Passell and Alfred E. Kahn have suggested that one solution for the local service problem is "measured service." The individual residential user might be charged a basic price for either a dial tone alone, or for a dial tone plus a few free calls each month — a "lifeline" option now available in California for $2.50 a month.[60] Eric J. Schneidewind, a member of the Michigan Public Service Commission, pointed out that recent federal decisions to raise long-distance rates would in fact raise lifeline rates to $10-to-$12 per month, with no free calls at all. Moreover, the equipment for offering that service to all customers would not be available from many large companies for several years, and smaller companies would have to wait even longer. Finally, Schneidewind declared, nonsubsidized measured service (the equivalent of having a pay phone in one's home) cannot work well unless all customers use it.[61]

On these matters, Passell's arguments indicate how confusing conventional analysis can be. The lowest cost per customer in a transportation system, whether humans, voices, or freight are being transported, can be achieved only when all customers use the same system. In the case of telephones, the measured-service equipment Passell endorses cannot logically be installed unless all phones use it. When he turns to evaluating the installation of airbags in automobiles, however, Passell uses an analytical scheme he rejected for telephones. He calculates that if airbags are installed in only a few thousand cars, as Mercedes-Benz decided to do, the cost is $1,000 per car, but, if installed in a few million cars, the cost drops to $300. Using the same approach, he advocates that government should also compel auto firms to install five-mile-per-hour bumpers on all cars. The theory at work here is an important modification of free-market theory. No single auto maker feels it can afford to take the lead in installing air bags and stronger bumpers, because individual customers might not choose to buy them. Moreover, no single customer can calculate how much tough bumpers and airbags are ultimately worth in repair savings or in reduced injuries. Thus, regulation overcomes the problem of insufficient information that always bedevils free-market decisions. Since the ultimate costs would be levied upon all citizens in the form of insurance premiums and highway taxes, Passell concludes that government is justified in intervening to reduce costs that cannot be allocated among individual customers.[62] The Passell who analyzes auto safety is wiser than the Passell who analyzes phones.

New telephone technologies have acted to obscure the very same problem in communications. New long-distance service can be installed between major cities, and even smaller ones; for this, customers are then charged much lower rates than in the old Bell System. The new companies, however, are under no obligation to provide pay phones on street corners or to serve rural areas. Meanwhile, the number of companies competing for long-distance customers on even the high-density routes makes the total costs of all new systems much higher than need be, because the new systems duplicate both the old Bell System and each other as well. Ultimately, this leads to higher rates than are necessary; and to additional social costs as a number of long-distance companies inevitably go bank-rupt, costs being transferred to society in the final analysis. Over time, it may be clear that this problem is not limited to telephone communications. Anyone familiar with the proliferation of uncoordi-nated and noninterfacing, computer-based information-retrieval systems understands that users will be unable to use all the infor-mation that is within the sum total of all such systems, just as government agencies that have designed and built noninterfacing computer systems (through competitive bidding) have found that they cannot quickly make their information available to each other.

A sad note may now be added. Moody's Investor Service decided in March of 1983 that it must lower the credit rating of AT & T and all but one of its subsidiaries and affiliates. Since the early 1960s, the corporation and all but two operating companies had been rated AAA – the highest possible rating. While he did not believe the reduction would have a "large" effect on rate payers, Moody's chief financial officer announced that technology and all-out competition would now compel the companies to pay higher interest rates on future borrowing. While other financial evaluators did not immediately follow Moody's lead, who could be sure this would be the last word in lower credit ratings?[63]

The deregulators may accomplish something they had not intended: In the near future, teenagers may find it too expensive to spend long hours on the phone talking with friends, and to this extent, even parents may initially applaud the system. If, however, driving becomes cheaper than calling, the same teenagers will do more visiting, and have more accidents. When seamless policy areas have broad social consequences, dividing them into watertight compartments for the sake of making sophisticated analyses can often lead to disaster.

SURVEYING THE DAMAGE

The careful reader of this chapter and the preceding one may note that, while I have provided numerous examples of bad decisions and bad outcomes, each chapter includes an example of a good decision and a good outcome. Garbage removal in Minneapolis was handled rather well, and so was the settlement of the dispute between basketball owners and players, even if all the participants in the two decision processes did not have, and doubtless do not have now, a complete picture of what happened and why. The Minneapolis scheme was prompted by the belief that local firms should not be summarily thrown out of business in favor of an outside company; and the basketball agreement emerged only as the league and many of its member teams approached total ruin. If crisis thinking, no matter its weaknesses, is an improvement upon economic theology, nothing will have been gained in the long run unless good examples are studied again and again.

While the Minneapolis decision can stand as an example of how to divide the business, it does not follow that it is necessary or desirable to turn over many public functions to private contractors. This is especially the case with the refuse-disposal industry, long believed to have connections with organized crime. A 1976 federal law provided the first regulation of toxic-waste handling, and subsequent investigations have shown that many refuse-disposal companies have done large-scale illegal dumping, and that they are indeed connected with organized crime. A local government could not be expected to investigate such matters before awarding contracts. Because the recent evidence includes bribery of officials and competitive bids, a part of the toxic-waste problem is likely traceable to the problems of competitive bidding.[64]

Sensible outcomes were achieved in these cases without severely disrupting anything except the classic theology. Put another way, each solution implicitly accepted the notion that legalized collusion or collective planning was preferable to maintaining a blind commitment to the free market. There is no reason to conclude that any of the parties to either agreement abdicated any of their responsibilities. There is every reason to believe that many such agreements could easily be worked out. The key, I think, is to realize that an agreement between government and contractors, and an agreement between owners and players, is a form of antitrust immunity. If an agreement were developed for each case requiring one, then every industry would then be exempt from the antitrust laws, and the laws would then be seen as the absurdities they always have been. As indicated, moreover, the correct form of regulation can vary from industry to industry, and need not always involve direct government regulation.

The mere reinstatement of the abandoned regulatory systems could not repair all the damage. In transportation and communications, efficiency can be achieved only by establishing a rule that a single company, no matter who may own or operate it, must provide service for a single route. This need not require that a single firm be assigned the task of serving all airline, truck, bus, rail, shipping, or communications routes. Indeed, multiple operations are useful for providing ways to measure comparative performances, but when passengers, voices, freight, or information must move along the routes served by a number of operators, then the systems themselves must be fully compatible with each other. Standardization, therefore, becomes important, not only for efficiency in movement, but also for safety reasons. The job of safety inspectors, for example, becomes exponentially more difficult as more and more types of aircraft, buses, trucks, and other vehicles make it impossible for them to adequately stay abreast of new developments. If, as Passell suggests, standardized automobile bumpers are a virtue, the suggestion has wider application.

Those dedicated to classical theology, of course, will not accept my assessment of what has occurred in deregulated industries. They will continue, at least for a time, to define disaster as success. Sooner or later, however, the larger breakthrough must come. Until this occurs, still other silly games will continue to play themselves out. I take up some of these games in the next chapter.

APPENDIX: AIRLINE-INDUSTRY DATA

Figures 1-4 are taken from public reports of the Civil Aeronautics Board. The compilations were prepared by the Financial and Cost Analysis Division of the Office of Economic Analysis, and were released on January 3, 1983. The data are rather self-explanatory with respect to how the entire airline industry has fared since deregulation took effect late in 1978. Such data are routinely ignored by those who proclaim the virtues of deregulation, including those in the U.S. Congress who pushed through the legislation.

As outlined earlier, the problems in this and other deregulated industries are routinely ascribed to factors other than the policy of deregulation itself. In scientific terms, the relationship between the adoption of a policy of deregulation and a downturn in the financial condition of the industry is not a correlation, but only a coincidence.

Because the Civil Aeronautics Board is, at the time of this writing, scheduled to be abolished in 1984, data of this sort may no

longer be available in the future. In the absence of legal require-
ments for providing such data to a regulatory agency, it will be
increasingly difficult to ascertain precisely what is happening. The
need of competitors to keep secrets from each other is one of the
greatest ironies of the discipline of economics. Its practitioners
pride themselves on their commitment to scientific methods and
empirical testing, yet they seek to promote competition to such an
extent that data become unavailable, or at best questionable because
there are no outside agencies to monitor the data.

FIGURE 1
Change in Working Capital (in $ billion), Total Certificated Industry

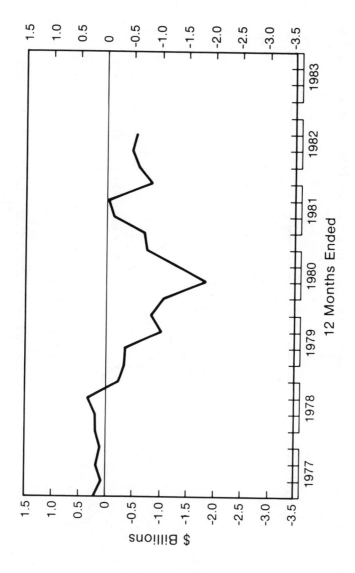

FIGURE 2
Major Fund Sources (Internal Sources and External Sources) (in $ billion), Total Certificated Industry

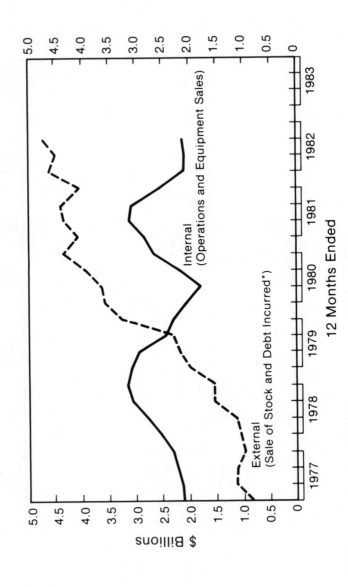

*Includes capitalized leases.

FIGURE 3
Long-Term Debt Incurred and Repayment of Long-Term Debt (in $ billion), Total Certificated Industry

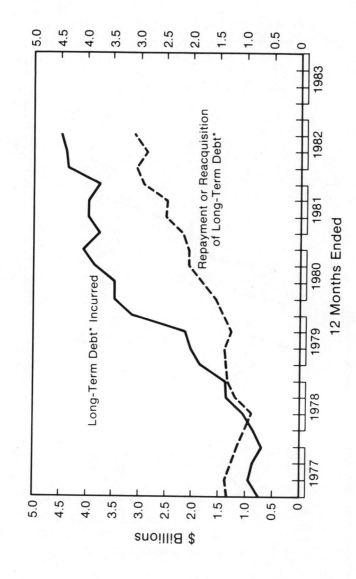

*Includes capitalized leases.

121

FIGURE 4
Current Ratio (as a percent), Total Certificated Industry

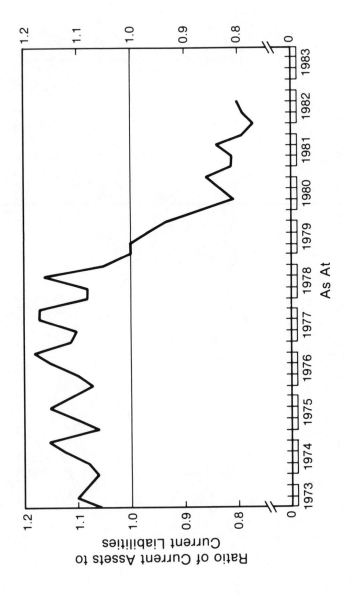

NOTES

1. Stephen Breyer, *Regulation and Its Reform* (Cambridge: Harvard University Press, 1982), pp. 198, 228.

2. Ibid., p. 209.

3. Ibid., p. 212.

4. U.S. Civil Aeronautics Board, "Petition of World Airways, Inc., for Emergency Rulemaking," Docket 40513 (Washington, D.C., March 9, 1982).

5. Milton and Rose Friedman, *Free to Choose* (New York: Avon Books, 1981), p. 190.

6. James C. Miller III, "A Perspective on Airline Regulatory Reform," *Journal of Air Law and Commerce* 41 (1975): 679, 690.

7. David Lloyd-Jones, "Deregulation and Its Potential Effect on Airline Operations," in ibid., p. 826.

8. U.S. Civil Aeronautics Board, *Report of the CAB Special Staff on Regulatory Reform* (Washington, D.C., 1975), pp. 206-22.

9. J. M. Ramsden, *The Safe Airline: How the Airline Industry Operates* (Brooklyn, N.Y.: Beekman, 1976), p. 185.

10. *New York Post*, June 30, 1982.

11. *Washington Post*, June 19, 1982 (letter to editor).

12. In one period, January-March 1982, the number of complaints per 100,000 passengers was as follows: Capitol, 43.2; People Express, 17.48; New York Air, 12.2; TWA, 6.2; US Air, 3.47; American, 3.15; Braniff, 2.9; United, 2.8; Eastern, 2.26; Delta, 0.9. U.S. Civil Aeronautics Board, *CAB News*, News Release 82-87 (Washington, D.C., 1982).

13. *CAB Special Staff Report*, pp. 6-7.

14. *New York Times*, May 1, 1983 (letter to business editor).

15. Ibid., June 6, August 21, and September 8, 1982.

16. *Washington Post*, July 16, 1982.

17. *New York Times*, June 22, 1982.

18. *Washington Post*, July 16, 1982.

19. Robert Mabley, "The Elusive Exit Rate," in *Conference on Regulatory Reform in Surface Transportation* (Preprint Papers) (Washington, D.C.: Department of Transportation, DOT-DMA-50/83/22, March 1983), pp. 104-13.

20. Breyer, op. cit., Chap. 12.

21. Ibid., p. 225.

22. Ibid., p. 228.

23. Ibid.

24. D. Daryl Wyckoff, *Truck Drivers in America* (Lexington, Mass.: Lexington Books, 1979), p. 120.

25. *New York Times*, July 2, 1979.

26. Andrew F. Popper, "Shipper Antitrust Liability in a Rate-Deregulated Market," in Grant M. Davis, ed., *Collective Ratemaking in the Motor Carrier Industry* (Danville, Ill.: Interstate Publishers, 1980), pp. 45-70.

27. *USA Today*, February 22, 1983.

28. *New York Times*, February 21, 1983.

29. *Wall Street Journal*, March 2, 1983.

30. *Washington Post*, September 4, 1982.

31. *New York Times*, January 14, 1983.

32. *USA Today*, April 27, 1983.

33. *Washington Post*, January 28, 1983.

34. *Sports Illustrated*, April 11, 1983, p. 13.

35. *Washington Post*, March 15, 1983.

36. *New York Times*, February 6, 1983.

37. Milton and Rose Friedman, op. cit., Chap. 3.

38. Charles M. Haar and J. Morton Davis, "Banks and the Economy," *New York Times*, August 9, 1982. Haar is a professor of law at Harvard; Davis is president of an investment banking firm.

39. Joseph Kraft, "Up Against the Interest Rates," *Washington Post*, July 11, 1982.

40. Martin Mayer, "Earn 100% at Mountebanks," *New York Times*, December 17, 1982.

41. *USA Today*, April 27, 1983, quoting two investment counselors. Admittedly, others believe the stock market "boom" is a signal of a recovery.

42. *New York Times*, January 28, 1983.

43. Ibid., May 8, 1983.

44. Susan Kaufman Purcell, "Banking on Mexico — Badly," in ibid., August 24, 1982.

45. I. J. Davis, "More Skinflints, Please," in ibid., October 29, 1982.

46. Hobart Rowen, "After the Penn Square Fiasco," *Washington Post*, July 15, 1982.

47. *New York Times*, March 10, 1983 (figures from Federal Reserve Board).

48. Ibid., March 8, 1983.

49. The post-Keynesians suggest that the "supportive" function of central banks is much more important than their "control" (of money supply) function. In a nutshell, one must first decide how a market system must be designed (regulated) before undertaking to manage the money supply. If unregulated supply (and all schools of economics accept this as desirable) is to be permitted, no system of money regulation can solve the resultant problems. See Alfred S. Eichner, *A Guide to Post-Keynesian Economics* (White Plains: M. E. Sharpe, 1978, 1979), esp. "Introduction" by Joan Robinson, and pp. 120-38.

50. Domenick Armentano, *Antitrust and Monopoly* (New York: John Wiley, 1982), p. 63.

51. *New York Times*, December 23, 1982 (letter to editor).

52. Interview with Gerard W. Mackworth-Young, of Morgan Grenfell & Co., *New York Times*, June 21, 1983.

53. Charles Peters, "Insure the Consumer," in ibid., December 31, 1982.

54. John Kenneth Galbraith, *The New Industrial State*, 2d ed. rev. (Boston: Houghton Mifflin, 1971), p. 358.

55. Ibid., p. 360.

56. *New York Times*, February 16, 1983.

57. Andrew J. Stein, "Get Ready for Phone Bills to Double," in ibid., April 24, 1983; Peter Passell, "Don't Hang the Phone Company Yet," ibid., March 28, 1983, *Pittsburgh Press*, June 25, 1983.

58. *Pittsburgh Press*, January 10, 1983.

59. "Bell's Long-Distance Battle," *New York Times*, October 13, 1982. Also see, *Wall Street Journal*, June 21, 1983.

60. Passell, op. cit.

61. *New York Times*, April 21, 1983 (letter to editor).

62. Peter Passell, "Airbags for Adam Smith," in ibid., May 10, 1983.

63. "Bell's Tarnished Debt Rating," in ibid., March 11, 1983.

64. See *New York Times*, June 5, 1983, p. 7.

6
Deficits:
How We Lie to Ourselves

The widely popular view is that public borrowing and spending, especially by the federal government, has kept interest rates high, thereby "drying up" the capital needed for investment in new plants and equipment. The view is not a unanimous one, even if congressional liberals and conservatives alike worry about increasing federal deficits. One dissenter, Robert B. Reich, notes that even today's federal debt is less than 30 percent of the gross national product (GNP), about what it was in the late eighteenth century. By the same token, other advanced countries (West Germany, Japan, and France) have long maintained a larger public debt than the United States, when measured as a percentage of GNP. And, Reich argues, the United States has not fallen significantly short of other countries in new plant investment.[1]

Another group of dissenters is the supply-siders, including both economists (Arthur Laffer) and politicians (Representative Jack Kemp of New York). They believe that large cuts in income taxes, while they produce substantial deficits for a time, encourage huge new investment in needed industrial expansion. This doctrine, expressed as: "a rising tide lifts all boats," holds that the expansion then vastly increases government revenues. In spelling out the doctrine, George Gilder[2] uses the example of England in the late eighteenth and early nineteenth centuries. Left with high deficits after a long period of war ending in Napoleon's defeat, the country entered a period of expansion. Even with low tax rates, tax revenues increased so much that deficits no longer were a problem. In referring only to Lord Macaulay's capsule history of England, Gilder overlooks important other evidence. Wartime prosperity gave way to a sudden depression after the war ended in 1815. Growth in the 1820s was followed by a very severe depression from 1836 to 1842. Income tax rates were indeed low or nonexistent during the expansion because, in that era, the income tax was used only as an emergency measure (during war, and then during the slump of the 1830s). Government depended primarily upon revenues from high tariffs and a plethora of sales, or user, taxes. Further, expansion was not steady, but occurred only in wildly fluctuating cycles. As the first industrialized country, England faced little competition for some of its output, yet was unable to manage stable growth. As dedicated classicists, the supply-siders believe that overexpansion is impossible, and believe that low income taxes (especially for the rich) stimulate investment. They even have criticized a conservative president (Reagan) for worrying too much about deficits. Both of these dissenting views correctly minimize the problem of government deficits, but incorrectly argue for huge new industrial investment. The data on p. 128 are worth close attention.

Responsibility for assembling the data shifted from the Commerce Department to the Federal Reserve Board after 1976. While the two agencies generally agreed on the amount of debt in other categories, they differed widely on the amount of corporate debt (see Table 1). In telephone conversations with officials of the two agencies, I was unable to get any clear explanation for the discrepancy (the Federal Reserve may have eliminated intercorporate debt, but this is not clear). If the Commerce Department was correct, corporate debt passed the $1 trillion mark in 1976, six years before the federal debt drew giant headlines for doing the same thing. Even using Federal Reserve data, moreover, the federal debt has become less and less important as a fraction of total debt, declining from approximately one-third in 1950 to less than one-sixth in 1981. Even if the combined debts of all governments are included, the public debt has been declining in significance. While corporate debt has been growing by leaps and bounds since World War II, it does not seem disproportional at first glance, provided the Federal Reserve's figures are more valid than those of Commerce. This may not be a reasonable assumption, because when one calculation is more than double another ($1.4 trillion vs. $.687 trillion in 1976), a safer approach is to split the difference. If the Federal Reserve

TABLE 1
U.S. Credit Market Debt, 1950-81
(in billions of dollars)

Debt Category	*Commerce Department Data*			
	1950	*1960*	*1970*	*1976*
Total debt	486	874	1,882	3,355
Government	240	308	485	833
Federal	217	240	301	516
Other	22	65	145	236
Corporations	142	303	797	1,415
Individuals	104	263	600	1,107
Mortgages	55	151	345	684
Consumers	22	56	127	218

	Federal Reserve Board Data					
	1960	*1970*	*1976*	*1979*	*1980*	*1981*
Credit-market debt	780	1,946	2,907	4,235	4,652	5,118
Government	308	522	754	958	1,063	1,173
Federal	236	341	516	664	743	830
Other	72	181	238	295	320	343
Corporations	154	458	687	972	1,062	1,177
Individuals	264	751	1,087	1,648	1,783	1,918
Mortgages	173	486	714	1,085	1,187	1,268
Consumers	65	178	249	383	385	414

Source: Bureau of the Census, *Statistical Abstract of the United States* (Washington, D.C.: Government Printing Office, 1982-83), p. 501.

is correct, however, corporate debt has been growing at about the same overall rate as the individual debt taken on for buying what is produced.

Reich's analysis assumes that the United States has invested about the correct amount in new plant and equipment, presumably because he thinks overinvestment is impossible. Since I suggest that the problem lies in too much investment in the making of things to sell, is there any evidence to support this view? While the subject can be approached within a U.S. context, it is likely that there has been excessive investment in new plant all around the world. It is misleading, then, to refer to "private-sector" investment as Americans are wont to do. If Zambia borrows from Western banks to develop copper mines, Americans would label this private-sector investment, but Zambia would describe it as something else, i.e., a government-managed "national development plan." But perhaps the question to be asked should be refined a bit. Is it possible that too much capital has been available to those who produce things to sell, whether those producers be in the United States or elsewhere?

Is this really an important question at all? The answer ultimately must depend upon the significance and implications of deficit spending, and here we arrive at one of the simplest but most far-reaching absurdities of economic theory. The widely held view is that only public borrowing is a problem because it depletes the amount of capital available for other borrowers, thus driving up the costs of "renting" money, i.e., interest rates. From a common-sense perspective, all borrowing, regardless of who is doing the borrowing, reduces the amount available for remaining borrowers, regardless of who else seeks to borrow. Thus, corporate borrowing can make capital scarce for government, thereby forcing the latter to levy new taxes for the purpose of paying the higher interest rates. In economic theory, the dubious double-entry bookkeeping of the private market makes only government borrowing a problem. The mythology is fascinating.

If a firm borrows money, it presumably does so in order to create "new wealth," because it uses the money either to build a plant or to operate existing plants, the money being transformed into plants and products that have market value. If a firm uses the money to buy another firm, this depletes the money capital of the buyer, but the seller now has new money to invest, so that all such exchanges do not, in principle, reduce the amount of capital available for still other borrowers. Note how easily the concept of equilibrium solves everything. While this is a slight oversimplification, each exchange presumably leaves each party at least as well off as before any transaction, but does this assumption really make any sense? It does, provided that all the plants and their outputs can be sold for at least the costs of building and production. Because overproduction is, in principle, impossible, any other outcome is impossible. But if overcapacity and overproduction are accepted as possible, then everyone cannot be sure of this, and, if overcapacity and overproduction are inevitable, as I argue, the bubble must burst. After all, what is a plant worth if its output cannot be sold?

The economic reasons for looking upon public borrowing as a problem seem to be two in number. The first is rather startling once it is thoroughly understood. If a corporation builds a new plant, it and the equipment are placed in a separate category in the national income accounts used to monitor how well the country is doing. Thus, when Reich and others refer to "investment," they have in mind the amount of money put to work making things to sell. If a government, on the other hand, borrows money to build a bridge or highway, this is *not* considered an investment, because the government seldom intends to sell what it builds. On this matter, the leading authority is Charles L. Schultze, formerly Jimmy Carter's chief economist:

> Part of federal, state and local government spending represents investment in productive assets (schools, highways, sewerage and water systems) which contribute to the capacity and efficiency of the economy. In the U.S. national income accounts, however, unlike those of most foreign countries, such investment-type outlays by government are not included in the investment category of GNP, which is reserved for private investment.[3]

If this seems absurd to you, it does to me as well. If a bridge and highway are needed to provide access to a new plant, the word "investment" would seem equally applicable to all three, but it is not, at least not in the United States. The result is both economically and politically disastrous; we deceive ourselves as to the meaning of investment calculations, and we perpetuate the myth that only private spending creates "wealth," while public spending creates only "waste."*

The second reason is that because government borrowing is not offset, on the other side of credit ledgers, by the market value of what government produces, the borrowing supposedly depletes the

---

*Small wonder that so many Americans trained in economics resist government ownership and operation of industries producing things to sell. To acknowledge that government could efficiently operate anything would threaten fundamental economic concepts. Similarly, American bookkeeping implies, and Americans generally believe, that business must be efficient because it, and it alone, creates wealth.

nation's wealth. From this perspective, government can only "monetize" its new debt by simply printing more money which, because it is not backed by anything of value, is worthless. In this way, so goes the argument, only public borrowing and spending fuel the engines of inflation. This accounts for the view that if inflation is to be curtailed, public spending must be reduced; and that because many public expenditures are almost beyond challenge, reductions (as in the 1980s) are imposed on social services.[4] The schizophrenia of economic theory (consumers vs. workers) makes it possible to overlook the fact that cuts in social programs have the effect of reducing purchasing power and demand.

The central question now beckons once again. What evidence might indicate that too much capital is available for what Americans label private-sector borrowing? I suggest that the answer lies in the "mergermania" of recent years, even if merger activity, more recently, may have been slowing down a bit. The reasons why the United States has experienced repeated periods of high merger activity are quite easy to understand, I further suggest, if one is not committed to economic theology. Mergers are the inevitable sequel to industrial overexpansion.

MERGERMANIA AT WORK

The first major merger movement in the United States occurred at the turn of the century, and it featured horizontal mergers within individual industries. Indeed, 78 percent of those mergers resulted in firms that produced 50 percent or more of the output of the individual industries.[5] It is not coincidental that the movement followed the severe depression of the 1890s, nor that the passage of antitrust laws accompanied the movement. The immediate question, however, is: What has been happening in recent years? Reich's assessment is that mergers recently have been occurring at a "breakneck pace," especially among what are called conglomerates. In 1977, American companies spent $22 billion in buying one another and, in 1979, $43.5 billion. The 1982 total was a staggering $82 billion. By this time, DuPont's expenditure of $7.5 billion to buy Conoco is famous, but not appreciably more so than the "Byzantine wheeling and dealing" involved in the Martin-Marietta struggle with Bendix. When the latter sought to take over the former, Martin-Marietta retaliated by seeking to take over Bendix. It was possible at one point that the management of each firm would take control of the other — an outcome averted only when a still larger conglomerate, Allied, merged with Bendix to save it from falling prey to a United Technologies takeover that would have helped Martin-Marietta.[6]

To understand why and how mergermania began in the mid-1960s and then reached epidemic proportions in the late 1970s, it is well to recall that during the long post-World War II boom, the large firms were in a position to assemble a great deal of investment capital in the form of retained earnings. Throughout most of this period, corporations financed expansion by using the money they had collected from consumers (taxes disguised as prices). In the normal scheme of things, the funds are used to build new plants so as to further increase a firm's output, which, in principle, can indeed be sold. If such investments do what they are supposed to do — create plants and jobs — hardly anyone questions them. Overexpansion, after all, is always thought impossible.

The first critical shift occurs when managers find that it is cheaper to buy other firms in the same industry than it is to build new plants. The telltale sign is that the stock market price of a firm falls below the book value of the firm; i.e., the total market value of all shares of stock is less than the assumed value of the firm's assets.[7] The question overlooked is why this happens, and the answer cannot be found in economic theory. Put simply, a plant whose output cannot be sold is worth little. When an existing plant can be purchased for less than it costs to build a new plant, the logical conclusion is that the industry has greater capacity than needed to meet market demand. The corollary is obvious: Managers have money to spend, but, since they cannot justify building new plants, they turn to buying other firms instead.

As outlined earlier, competition among the large firms in an oligopoly compels each manager to seek to maintain or increase his share of the total market for a product. The accompanying managerial argument is that if one firm buys another in the same industry, new economies of scale will result. Managerial staffs can be consolidated, raw-materials purchases combined, and new technologies more easily adopted. The argument is superficially attractive, in that 50 state governments might be able to buy typewriters at a lower cost if they consolidated purchases. The argument doesn't stand up well,* but it is enough to note that such mergers are attractive only because used assets are cheaper to buy, and it is over-capacity that makes them cheaper.

What is slowing down this form of horizontal merger more than ever before is the fear that the Justice Department will disallow mergers by declaring them "overconcentrations" of market power. It is not important to know how the trust busters go about deciding that a merger should be overruled because calculations show that the new firm's percentage market share will be too high; it is only important to know that the trust busters do this. In recent merger wars, many proposed mergers were abandoned because the Justice Department (or the Federal Trade Commission) indicated disapproval. On the basis of long and hard experience, firms knew that even if they succeeded in overturning such decisions, they would be the losers. It was widely believed, for example, that when DuPont, Seagram, and Mobil were seeking to acquire Conoco, a Mobil-Conoco merger would be disallowed.

When a corporation has money to invest, but feels it cannot invest in new plants (due to no demand) and cannot buy another firm in the same industry (antitrust problems), what else is there to do except buy a firm in some other industry? This is by far the simplest and most persuasive explanation for the growth of conglomerates in the past 15 years. It is overlooked only because it does not conform to classical principles. The participants in merger wars are indeed corporate giants, for the most part. They have profits they cannot distribute as greatly increased dividends, for share-holders would then expect the same returns every year. The saddest thing to observe is the attempt to explain in managerial gobbledygook why it makes sense for a firm to buy another firm that the first firm knows absolutely nothing about.

When heterogeneous mergers take place, it is impossible to claim that economies of scale will produce new efficiencies. Indeed, close

---

*Losing $21 million in 1980, Continental Airlines was a troubled firm, and Texas International (a much smaller firm) then sought to buy it. Yet the prevailing view was, and is, that no significant economies of scale exist in the industry. Economists who supported the merger (nobody protested) thus forgot the argument of economists favoring deregulation. Often, these were the same economists.

analysis would show that managerial staffs must expand, with layer upon layer being added to manage the exceedingly diverse corporate empires. The most prominent argument is that conglomerates are "synergistic," which, in everyday language, means that "the whole is greater than the sum of its parts." In some mystical way, the product mix is thought to make all members of a conglomerate more profitable than each member would be on its own. "Synergy" is the handiest of claims; since nobody can precisely define its characteristics, nobody can prove it is a sham.

Occasionally, "synergy" seems meaningful at first glance. After all, when Philip Morris and Miller Brewing are united, there is already an established linkage of cigarettes and beer. Very quickly, however, things become absurd. Did anyone really believe that when Mobil bought Montgomery Ward, the president of the oil company would be able to improve the marketing of underwear? How can the Chief Executive Officer of ITT be expected to keep up with bread baking and gardening? If he is to effectively supervise Wonder Bread and Burpee Lawn and Garden Products (and ITT owns both), isn't that his job? Even though we have institutes and training programs built around the notion of conglomerate synergy, it is all nonsense. Steeped in freshman economics and the offerings of business schools (e.g., strategic planning), some junior executives become acquisition experts who decide what firms conglomerates should buy, using as twin guidelines the notion that economic theory makes sense and that synergy is the lifeblood of management.

A firm whose stock price falls below the supposed money value of its assets is a likely target for an "unfriendly" takeover. When firm 1 seeks to take over firm 2, the attempt is "unfriendly" if firm 1 announces that it will get rid of firm 2's management. A "friendly" approach, conversely, is when firm 1 announces that it needs and will continue to employ firm 2's management. This is important only because merger wars become highly competitive and, just as in baseball, a poor performer can become the beneficiary of the competitive struggle. Indeed, any number of metaphors make sense. Once a firm becomes the focus of attention, many firms may enter the competition, if only out of fear that they will not "keep up with the Joneses." This much resembles the history of colonialism, with each colonial power acquiring colonies because it was important to stay even with, or ahead of, competitors. When a merger war begins to escalate, truly crazy things happen.

Remember that a firm becomes an attractive target for acquisition when its stock price indicates it can be bought at bargain-basement prices. Once the bidding war begins, however, things change. For example, at the height of the fight over Conoco, Mobil offered $115 per share to Conoco shareholders. This was 2½ times the lowest value of the stock during the previous year, and 25 percent above the value of the stock on the day of the offer. As the struggle proceeded, the bidders apparently lost sight of the fact that the bidding itself had made it virtually certain that by the time the war was over, Conoco would be no "bargain" at all. Deeply involved in its contest with Seagram and Mobil, DuPont could not know that, in plain language, it was the victim of a "sting." In the euphoric world of "paper entrepreneurialism,"[8] con games are everyday occurrences, not because the business world is full of con men, but because the environment compels managers to cheat each other.

The extent of the gamesmanship and cheating cannot be overstated. When a "hostile" formal offer is made, the defending firm, whose managers know their careers will end if the offer is successful, has precisely 20 days to locate a "white knight" who will agree to buy it. As an army of financial consultants sweeps the country to brief prospective "white knights," the managers, fearing for their professional lives, take to weaving "golden parachutes" for themselves. In military jargon, these are "contingency plans"; if the "hostile" buyer becomes successful, the deposed managers will have lucrative guaranteed contracts that will enable them to retire in luxury. "White knights" are chosen because they have money to spend (retained earnings), are able to borrow billions more, and cannot logically invest in new plants. The financial consultants reap huge rewards if they persuade a "white knight" to buy (First Boston won a $14-million commission from DuPont in the Conoco caper, while Conoco paid Morgan Stanley $14 million), but relatively little if they do not ($250,000). The company that agrees to be the "friendly" buyer has to make a very quick decision, and instantaneously borrow billions to take over another company in a business it knows nothing about.[9]

Small wonder that many of the "friendly" mergers become disasters for those who do the buying. After General Electric bought Utah International (a natural-resource company) in 1975, GE's shareholders lost (by 1982) an amount equal to 33 percent of GE's market value in 1975 and 150 percent of Utah's purchase price.[10] After U.S. Steel bought Marathon Oil, the former had to sell its office building and a number of subsidiaries to meet interest payments on the funds borrowed for the takeover.[11] DuPont has been suffering since it acquired Conoco, and so has Seagram, which, as one of the bidders for Conoco, ended up with a 20 percent interest in DuPont.[12] The patterns are remarkably similar across the board. The shareholders of the firm being sold reap great profits because the bidding wars suddenly change an undervalued firm (where stock is worth less than assets) to an overvalued firm (stock is worth more than assets). In this craziest of worlds, the firm most obviously in distress (the one that is sold) ultimately drags down the one presumably in better shape (the buyer).

While there is a lingering unhappiness with mergermania, those who attack it miss the larger point. Lisle C. Carter, Jr., a university president serving as a director of Heublein, gave up his job by voting for a merger with R. J. Reynolds (a case of the synergy of whiskey and tobacco). Decrying the "draining" effects of a merger war in which Reynolds won out over General Cinema, he suggested that mergers should be made much more difficult to consummate.[13] Edgar M. Bronfman, himself an inveterate merger warrior as chairman of Seagram, concluded that tax deductions should no longer be allowed on money borrowed to buy other companies; if the economists did not recognize that all this borrowing contributed something to high interest rates, this practicing executive did understand it.[14] A number of members of Congress, and the Justice Department, have hoped for some years to limit merger activity because it threatens to lead to too much concentration and to still further limitations on all-out competition. Since conglomerate acquisitions do not by themselves immediately decrease the number of firms in any industry, it is small wonder that an antitrust case cannot easily be made against them. While no clear doctrine has emerged for disallowing conglomerate mergers, the Supreme Court declared illegal, in 1967, the 1957 acquisition of Clorox by Procter & Gamble, which was not in the household-liquid-bleach market (Clorox accounted for half the market). A former solicitor general, cites the case in arguing that conglomerate mergers, because they do not injure competition, should always be permitted. As I shall indicate, this is precisely the reason they should be prohibited.[15]

One unusual criticism of mergers turns upside down a secondary argument often made in their favor. When U.S. Steel bought

Marathon, much was said about the desirability of "diversification" for the steel producer. This is much like the situation of a developing country whose prosperity and balance-of-trade payments depend almost exclusively upon a single natural resource or agricultural commodity. Two analysts have concluded, after careful study, that conglomerate mergers represent attempts by conglomerate managers to diversify the risk of their becoming unemployed. A manager, for example, has only a single employer (the conglomerate) but, if there is enough variety in the collection of companies he supervises, it is unlikely that all of them will fail.[16] To that I would add that if market share is the managerial test within an industry, sheer size is the only standard for determining if one conglomerate is staying abreast of its competitors. In the gamesmanship of merger wars, of course, size measured by a firm's inflated asset value can be extraordinarily misleading.

The gradual increase in merger activity during the mid-1960s, followed by the frenetic increases of the late 1970s and early 1980s, corresponds closely to what could be expected by the use of the theory argued in this book. As European and Japanese industry rebuilt, and as developing countries launched their industrial plans, overcapacity gradually, and then rapidly, made established companies decline in value. Because conglomerate mergers had the effect of propping up failing companies, they prevented more consolidation and regulation within individual industries. It is a measure of national and international confusion that so few understand that conglomerate mergers intensify competition rather than limiting it — the worst possible outcome. The longer all-out competition is intensified and sustained, the more dizzying must be the ultimate fall. A corollary rule, therefore, is that the greater the conglomerate-merger activity, the closer we approach a steep depression.

Standing alone, this would imply that the slight falloff in merger-mania in 1983 indicated that better days lay ahead. But, following the theory outlined herein, this cannot be so. As indicated earlier, Washington policy-makers have encouraged individuals to save more and more, but, because new plant investment makes little sense in an era of a capacity glut, the savings have been used to inflate stock prices. As the stock market began soaring in early 1983, many observers took this as a sign of an emerging recovery — an absurdity on at least two counts: If inflation is a problem, as so many insist, then continually inflating stock prices also must be a problem.

But, given the schizophrenia of economic theory, those who own stocks seek higher prices for what they can sell, but lower prices for everything they buy. Secondly, the same observers fail to note that when stock prices rise in the absence of huge new plant investment, things simply cannot be getting better.

In an era of overcapacity and a looming depression, stock markets become, more than ever, full-fledged gambling casinos. A troubled firm becomes a "good bet" because its stock price can be expected to soar if conglomerates fight over its possession. A firm showing promise may experience sudden increases in its stock price just before overcapacity in the industry leads to a plunge. Volatility reached such a point by mid-1983 that a booming new industry had emerged. Stock gamblers were investing in "stock-index futures," betting that hypothetical stock portfolios (as measured by the Standard & Poor or the New York Stock Exchange index) would quickly rise or fall. Essentially, these operate much like commodities-futures markets, but the bettors have no commitments to buy outputs; they are "playing the numbers." In March 1983, these futures had become the fastest-growing new contracts ever offered for sale on a commodities exchange.[17]

This brings us full circle to the question of deficits. Merger wars are conducted in part with retained earnings, and also involve the borrowing of billions upon billions. While a classical economist might distinguish between the impact of a line of credit and the borrowing of cash, this seems open to question. In each of the merger wars, all the competitors must assemble extensive lines of credit before they enter the fray. Billions in credit are then tied up while the "raiders" and the "white knights" joust on the battlefield, and the interest rates are very high for all the participants. Indeed, the greatest merger activity has coincided with peak interest rates, though a cause-effect relationship need not be assumed. Inevitably, however, the cost of the borrowing must be added to the prices charged consumers, thereby sustaining inflation. When all the costs of merger wars are tallied up, improvements in efficiency would have to be astronomical in order to compensate for those costs.

The policy questions, then, are relatively few, but cannot be handled without a reversal in thinking. If borrowing by some lenders makes it more difficult for others, there seems no reason to assume that only public deficits disrupt the economy. Whether the focus is banks or corporations, many of the assets carried on balance sheets (certainly a misnomer) are worth little or nothing. The euphoria of high-stress merger wars mistakenly gives the impression that firms worth very little only a few weeks earlier have suddenly become highly valuable. The consultants who peddle troubled firms to friendly buyers combine the best of motives (synergy), with considerable "get-rich-quick" talk mixed in, but, since the shareholders of firms being sold usually make out very well, some consultants and the managers who have insured their own survival can boast that they have served the interests of their shareholders. William Agee, the Bendix president who first went after Martin-Marietta, then found himself embroiled in a searing battle, and issued himself, and 15 executive colleagues, $15.7 million in "golden parachutes"; Agee's own contract guaranteed him $805,000 annually through 1987.[18] Since Bendix ultimately had to "surrender" to Allied, Agee did not last long there. Yet he insisted that the whole escapade would "improve the value of the [Bendix] shareholder's investment over the long term."[19] Since conglomerate mergers merely fuel inflation while contributing nothing to management improvements and, indeed, making a depression more likely, should they be banned on that score? The answer to the question becomes a bit more obvious once it is realized that such mergers are spawned by antitrust laws that prevent more sensible regulation from having an opportunity to emerge. Indeed, Justice Department lawyers spend their time hastily calculating such things as whether the merger of two beer companies will lead to overconcentration.*

Historically, overcapacity and depression led first to horizontal mergers and, as in the example of the steel industry, only this type of merger makes sense. American steel executives, echoing the ideas advanced in the Great Depression and earlier, constantly imply and informally request that antitrust laws be eased so as to permit more mergers in the industry. If this is not allowed, and if government does not protect the industry by limiting steel imports, some executives warn that they will have to join foreign-government-controlled companies in order to survive at all.[20] If horizontal mergers are to replace conglomerate warfare, however, the corollary

---

*In one recent beer merger, the winner (Stroh) was forced to agree to swap plants with Pabst (not involved), so as to ensure that the geographic distribution of beer competition would please antitrusters.

question is whether this will require some form of regulation, perhaps even government's direct involvement. Contrary to textbook economics and antitrust mythology, horizontal mergers have served the country better than conglomerate wars.

The basic problem remains: Merger wars occur because firms have been able to assess hidden taxes upon consumers, thereby raising mountains of capital for which they can find no other purpose. The nonconsumers contribute also, because government (regardless of which party controls it) frets so much over public deficits that everyone from schoolchildren to the old and infirm are taxed by having their benefits cut. When a Washington policymaker declares ketchup a "vegetable" for the sake of economizing on school lunches, he is seeking to make more money available for merger wars, even if he doesn't realize as much. Is it necessary, then, to revise the definition of "excess," or "windfall," profits? The answer obviously must be yes, because this is the most extreme of possible cases, indeed a worst-case situation. In a competitive market, industries overbuild to begin with; merger wars indicate that overbuilding already has gone so far that even corporate managers know that they cannot spend more on new plant capacity.

The available evidence is clear. Savings have not declined, but business investment dropped 5.5 percent in 1982, and was expected to drop another 3.1 percent in 1983, the first back-to-back decline in this country since World War II.[21] When retained earnings exceed the amount that can be used for new plant capacity in any firm's own industry, and can only be used to participate in merger wars, the earnings are more accurately defined as excess, or windfall, profits. They are a form of surplus tax revenues, which even if levied (as prices) and collected in good faith, should now be diverted to other uses, for example, public works.

The question of excess profits is one of morality, not merely economics and politics, and the question has been so defined by the staunchest advocates of capitalism. U.S. Congressman Jack Kemp praised *Wealth and Poverty*, the book that popularized supply-side economics, for demonstrating the "moral as well as practical merits of capitalism." Its author, even berating Adam Smith for having "put altogether too much emphasis upon self-interest rather than altruistic creativity as the foundation of the system," outlined the moral justification for entrepreneurialism:

Capitalism begins with giving . . . the Capitalists of primitive society were tribal leaders who vied with one another in giving great feasts. Similarly, trade began with offerings from one family to another or from one tribe to its neighbors. The gifts, often made in the course of a religious rite, were presented in hopes of an eventual gift in return. The compensation was not defined beforehand. . . . It is the willingness of man to give — or work — without a specific reward that allows liberty . . . gifts or investments are experimental in that the returns to the giver are unknown . . . the capitalist, by giving before he takes, pursues a mode of thinking and acting suitable to uncertainty . . . gifts will succeed only to the extent that they are altruistic and spring from an understanding of the needs of others. They depend upon faith in an essentially fair and responsive humanity.[22]

Supply-side philosophy links capitalism to selflessness, not self-ishness. This is a substantial (and, to a point, welcome) modification of Western individualism. Limitless profits can be justified, however, only if there is limitless demand. Yet even Robert Mundell, a supply-side economist, has acknowledged that demand cannot be infinite (see Chapter 1). For this reason, it must follow that profits are not only excess, but are immoral, when they cannot be used for new investment. The deeper issue, moreover, is not confined to capitalism. The function of Soviet managers, as their textbooks proclaim, is one of "raising the profit to assets ratio," presumably for the betterment of society.[23] The ultimate question is: who decides? Keynesianism can be interpreted as a doctrine of consumer sovereignty (consumers know best, and should be supported) closely aligned with Adam Smith's original philosophy; supply-siders would leave decision-making to those who offer "gifts" in the hope of garnering profits; and Marxists would rely upon the altruism of a worker dictatorship. As I suggested earlier, these are doctrines of authority that are much more similar than different.

Whatever their schools of thought, all economists content themselves with a vague hope that when a selling firm's shareholders reap their huge profits, they will invest in something useful. Yet the record seems clear that with new plants unneeded virtually across the board,* billions and billions are moving around in markets

---

*Technically, this is not completely correct. When new technology or industries emerge, investment makes sense. But if all those capable of high-tech

where those dollars are unneeded, with paper profits piling up. Those asking government to tax this money make only the minimum of recommendations. Their recommendations, along with those for reregulating interest rates, remain largely ignored, even though the suggestions come from sources that cannot be labeled radical.

Nothing can occur until the applicable parts of economic theory are abandoned. The logic of mergers is easy to understand, but only when an observer casts off the economic blinders. If huge amounts of capital are not needed for new plants, then making more and more capital available simply compels managers to look for something to do with it. In the present case, so much capital has been recently made available that an escalating stock market has put merger wars into remission. But even this cannot be understood without abandoning the old theories. The excuse for merger wars has been the presence of undervalued companies, but the rising stock market has made these companies appear less troubled than they really are. What has been labeled "incorrectly undervalued" should have been labeled "correctly valued as nearly worthless," and what is now perceived as a healthy market should be seen as a market full of "correctly overvalued" firms.

PUBLIC VS. PRIVATE DEFICITS

As the congressional debate on the federal budget proceeded in the spring of 1983, some leading Democrats made their positions clear. They contended that currently projected federal-deficit spending would "drain huge amounts of savings from the economy, drive up interest rates and choke off economic recovery."[24] To be sure, no debate in Washington can be isolated from all the other related issues. Many Democrats wanted to delay or rescind the third year of a tax-cut package that, beginning in 1981, had generally favored upper-income taxpayers at the expense of others. And, while Democrats seemed miscast in the role of seeking lower deficits and higher taxes (a supposed reversal of typical Democratic stances), President Reagan had been pursuing his own revenue-raising gambits, most of them labeled "user fees." Hardly anyone in Washington, nonetheless,

---

development proceed without regulation, overexpansion and a collapse take little time to run their course, as in the case of home computers.

was any longer ready to argue that federal-deficit spending was not a problem at all, but so I argue here. Even Socialist President Mitterand of France has blamed U.S. federal deficits for the world's economic problems, asserting they cause the high interest rates. Larger debts incurred to build industrial capacity apparently did not concern him.[25] From the preceding argument, it follows that if deficit spending is to be seen whole, public deficits cannot be looked at in isolation. The problem may not be that, as Democrats argued, federal borrowing would absorb more than half of all credit-market funds in 1984; but, rather, that the limiting of federal borrowing to only half the available funds was a sign that excessive funds would be left for the needless capers of financial manipulators.

While much of the argument should be clear by now, it is worth repeating that this argument for increased public borrowing and spending does not at all correspond with the old nostrums, attributed to Keynesian economics, that government should run high deficits when times are bad, and generate surpluses (the equivalent of profits) in good times. Because Keynesianism is connected only with demand stimulation, it has never been a reliable guide for what is needed, and today's Keynesians are of no more help than those who used it in previous decades to save the discipline of economics.

The argument is a twofold one and quite simple. First, while many would chafe over the loss of what Americans customarily label freedom, borrowing and spending for the purpose of making things to sell, typified by the American definition of investment, must be restricted. In a very general way, rises in public borrowing and spending should be offset by declines in corporate borrowing and spending, so that total deficit spending need not be substantially affected. The second part of the argument is, if anything, even simpler. It is quite possible that if the same standards were used to measure public and corporate financial activity, one of two outcomes would follow. Either federal deficits would become inconsequential or even nonexistent, or corporate deficits would be much higher than indicated by current data. The chief witnesses on this matter are themselves economists, even if they might not accept my larger argument.

Albert T. Sommers is senior vice president and chief economist of The Conference Board (formerly the National Industrial Conference Board), and he puts it this way:

Unlike a business [the federal government] treats its capital outlays as ordinary expense, including their purchase in its operating statement, setting up no depreciation reserve for their replacement, and calculating no net worth as the security against the government's debt. While special analyses in the budget identify some spending as of a capital nature, the analyses are retrospective and have no apparent influence on the planning of government outlay. A purchase of long-term assets adds to the deficit; a sale of assets reduces the deficit. If the same accounting practices were pursued by businessmen, the fastest-growing and potentially most successful businesses — those that are investing more than their depreciation charges — would show a deficit or markedly lower profits, while declining businesses that are investing less than their depreciation charges would show higher profits. For A.T.&T., for instance, conversion to government accounting would have reduced 1981 profits before taxes from $19 billion to $9 billion; for IBM, the reduction would have been from $9 billion to $2 billion. Both companies would have had to cut their capital outlay by about 50 percent to achieve their 1981 reported profits before taxes. Most small, fast-growing, high-technology companies would report totally illusory deficits year after year. In such an accounting structure, a company that sells a subsidiary, even at far below its book value, would show a tidy profit on the transaction. The federal deficit is conceptually equivalent to the change in its outstanding debt. By this measure, A.T.&T. has run a sizable deficit in every recent year.[26]

In arguing against the attempt in 1982 to enact a "budget-balancing" constitutional amendment, Alan S. Blinder of Princeton took a slightly different tack, reaching similar results:

Economists have been arguing for years that most of what we count as interest expense on the national debt during inflationary times really should be counted as repayment of principal. The reason is simple. Lenders realize that the purchasing power of their principal will be eroded by inflation. As compensation, they demand higher interest rates which, in effect, force borrowers to repay part of the principal early.

Since the government historically has paid a "real interest rate" (that is, the excess of the interest rate over the inflation rate) of only about 1 percent, the vast majority of what now appears in the budget as interest expense should really be counted as repayment of principal, according to this logic. And this logic, by the way, is precisely what the Financial Accounting Standards Board prescribed several years ago in its inflation-accounting standards for private businesses. Which accounting treatment is implied by the amendment: the inflation-accounting procedures of the FASB, or the outmoded procedures currently followed by the government? The answer is of some importance because, according to FASB definitions, the government has run a budgetary surplus during most of the past 20 years.[27]

Sommers's argument is that budgetary practices should be changed to clearly distinguish between *capital* (investment) and *operating* budgets — an approach that seems to be attracting wider support in Washington. The argument has the virtue of recognizing that public-works investments are important and necessary; and, because they lead to the construction of valuable assets (even if those assets never will be sold), they are worthy of deficit financing. In Sommers's view, new forms of double-entry bookkeeping would show this type of spending to be offset by the "net worth" of the construction, while enabling Washington policy makers to "withstand political demands for still further growth of current transfer payments." Blinder, conversely, implies that the only necessary correction is to count government interest payments as largely the repayment of principal. While the two approaches are generally compatible, both fall short, Sommers's more than Blinder's.

We are long overdue in recognizing that a public bridge is an investment, often a more necessary one than the plant facilities that rely upon it. Yet it remains the case that the money to pay off the debt must ultimately come from taxpayers in one form or another, just as corporations charge customers for the costs of construction. A separation of capital and operating budgets might have the effect of disguising the former, just as occurs in the private sector. Many are startled and angry now, for example, that electric-power companies seek permission, often successfully, to include, in the rates they charge customers, the capital they need for new plants. Those complaining the loudest, often consumer groups, seem unaware that corporations have always done the same thing. And, if Sommers is wholly aware of the importance of public works as investments, he seems inclined to deny transfer payments to those who need them, especially those who must, given the way policy-makers look at things, remain unemployed for the sake of stabilizing wages and salaries.* It is reasonable to conclude that if the federal budget is separated into capital and operating categories, only capital deficits will be politically acceptable.

As full-fledged members of the economics fraternity, both Sommers and Blinder miss the larger point. If they were to acknowledge that corporations vastly overborrow and overspend — because any other outcome is impossible in a competitive market system — they would then have to admit that corporate debt in this country, and similar types of debt elsewhere, now greatly exceed, and have often greatly exceeded, any level that could be labeled reasonable. Contrary to what economists prefer to believe, the amount of excessive debt may easily be measurable. It simply must be proportional to the amount of industrial overcapacity existing at any given time, although excess capacity could (or should) never be wholly eliminated, under any circumstances. As must one day be recognized, however, focusing on deficits is of only secondary importance. The misguided views about current deficits, public and private, are the result of a failure to recognize that we spend too much to build what we should not, while spending too little to build what we should.

Because the larger problems and the solutions to them must in the long run be simple to understand, if less easy to implement, it is enough to note that there is substantial evidence that indicates that public deficits are not a problem at all. This does not mean that whatever government does in any country is accomplished with the utmost efficiency, for this must forever be impossible in any organizational design that depends upon any form of top-down authority. The American belief that government is inefficient and business is efficient, however, could not be wider of the mark. Any monopoly, public or private, has all the incentive it needs to be as efficient as possible. While the manager of a competitive enterprise believes he has every incentive to be as efficient as possible, this does not matter since competition, within a society or globally, is socially inefficient by definition, greater competition always making things worse.

---

*This is not technically correct. More attention is paid to restricting blue-collar wage increases than to executive-salary increases, at least until companies suffer severe losses. By the time salaries are cut back, large numbers of workers usually have been laid off.

The ultimate insanity of economic theory, as it relates to public and private deficits, is that it is unwittingly dedicated to the proposition that the whole is *less* than the sum of its parts. The fiction is that as firms tax (customers) and borrow and spend to build plants or buy other firms, everyone becomes slightly richer than before. The fact is that as more and more is built, everything built is worth less and less. Meanwhile, anything government builds is labeled as worthless, and those (bureaucrats) who manage what government builds are scorned because the assets are unproductive. Important bookkeeping changes would wipe away some of the fog on our glasses, but that is not enough.

NOTES

1. Robert B. Reich, *The Next American Frontier* (New York: Times Books, 1983), p. 120.

2. George Gilder, *Wealth and Poverty* (New York: Basic Books, 1981), chap. 18.

3. Charles L. Schultze, *National Income Analysis* (Englewood Cliffs: Prentice-Hall, 1964), p. 28.

4. John Kenneth Galbraith, *Economics and the Public Purpose* (Boston: Houghton Mifflin, 1973), p. 192.

5. J. Fred Weston, *Mergers and Economic Efficiency* (Washington, D.C.: Government Printing Office, 1981), chap. 2.

6. Reich, op. cit., pp. 147-49.

7. Ibid., p. 146.

8. Ibid., chap. 8.

9. Leslie Wayne, "The Corporate Raiders," *New York Times Magazine,* July 19, 1982.

10. Wolf Weinhold, "The GE-Utah Lesson," *New York Times,* April 17, 1983.

11. *Pittsburgh Post-Gazette,* April 5, 1983.

12. "DuPont's Unconvincing Merger," *New York Times,* November 14, 1982.

13. Lisle C. Carter, Jr., "Making Company Takeovers Harder," in ibid., November 13, 1982.

14. Edgar M. Bronfman, "End the Tax Subsidies for Corporate Mergers," in ibid., September 29, 1982.

15. Weston, op. cit., chap. 5. See also, Robert H. Bork, *The Antitrust Paradox* (New York: Basic Books, 1979).

16. Yakov Amihud and Baruch Lev, "Risk Reduction as Managerial Motive for Conglomerate Mergers," *Bell Journal of Economics* 12 (Autumn 1981): 605-17.

17. *Pittsburgh Press* (from *Los Angeles Times*, May 29, 1983).

18. Jerry Knight, "Golden Parachutes Reward Corporate Failure," *Washington Post*, September 13, 1982.

19. William Agee, "Corporate Mergers' Value," *New York Times*, October 19, 1982.

20. *Pittsburgh Press*, April 30, 1983.

21. *Wall Street Journal*, June 23, 1983.

22. George Gilder, *Wealth and Poverty* (New York: Basic Books, 1981), pp. 21-27; quote from Congressman Kemp is on dust jacket; reference to Adam Smith is at p. x.

23. D. Gvishiani, *Organisation and Management* (Moscow: Progress Publishers, 1972), p. 117.

24. *New York Times*, May 10, 1983.

25. *New York Times*, May 18, 1983.

26. Albert T. Sommers, "The Federal Budget Should Be Rebuilt From the Ground Up," *Across the Board* (New York: The Conference Board, May 1981), p. 19.

27. Alan S. Blinder, "Vaudeville on the Potomac," *Washington Post*, August 27, 1982.

7
Setting the Agenda

To many Americans, whether teaching in universities or working in factories, the word "regulation" evokes about the same response as the word "committee." Both are considered evils best avoided, because free markets and individual choice are thought to be ideals not subject to question. Individualism, unfortunately, becomes authoritarianism when put to work in a social environment. Even so, serious observers conclude that on the one hand, because authority "is one way of expressing care for others," there is a "persistent fear that we will be deprived of this experience,"[1] and, on the other hand, that people in general have a "hunger" for the "compelling and creative leadership" that inspires them to "fight," "march," and sometimes "die" in its service.[2] Because the philosophy of individualism is based more upon dominance than submission, the dislike for regulation and committees expresses the fear of losing authority.

In this context, economic regulation often appears to be an undesirable imposition by one authority (government) that removes the authority of everyone else (producers and consumers). Similarly, social regulation of safety and health standards can appear to be an equally unwise intervention that removes the authority of a producer (to run his business in the way he believes will best "care" for customers) or, alternatively, as a necessary intervention that prevents one authority (the firm) from effectively removing the authority of others (consumers). These beliefs, I think, account for widespread opposition to economic regulation, which seemingly

149

threatens the authority of both producers and consumers, and for the divided opinion on social regulation.

The opposition to economic regulation depends largely upon the presumed perfection, or at least near-perfection, of free markets. Nobel laureate George Stigler, for example, outlines the deficiencies of economic regulation by contrasting them with the "known" benefits of consumer sovereignty and competition.[3] By definition, an ideal cannot be improved upon, so that anything which appears to interfere with steady progress toward attainment of that ideal must only make things worse. This accounts for the many attempts, throughout American history, to combine presumably undesirable and reluctantly accepted economic regulation with as much competition as possible. When this turns out not to work well, the idealists then proclaim that still *more* competition is needed when, in reality, the only solution is *less* competition. Only when it is understood that free markets cannot work under any and all conditions will it then be acknowledged that economic regulation is needed everywhere. The evidence in this book, incomplete though it may be, suggests that economic regulation is the normal state of affairs, not the occasional and temporary exception, and that it is a prerequisite for effective social regulation. From this perspective, the single most prominent argument against regulation can be laid to rest.

THE ABSURD THEORY OF "CAPTURE"

The dominant view is that any regulatory agency is, virtually without exception, "captured" by the firms it regulates. The "capture" theory turns up in Supreme Court decisions written by the liberal Justice William Douglas, in the criticisms of the conservative economist George Stigler, and in the muckraking of Ralph Nader,[4] and is so widely accepted in academe that anyone believing otherwise is thought to be "hopelessly naive or even disingenuous."[5] The liberal solution for this capture is a set of tougher and more detailed safety and health standards, combined with rigorous antitrust enforcement of competition — a combination believed necessary to protect consumers from corporate capture. Where economic regulation is concerned, the solution for both liberals and conservatives is to remove regulation and encourage competition. Conservatives, including business people, dislike economic regulation (except when, as members of a particular industry, they seek protection); and liberals believe that regulators, by protecting established firms, enable those firms to accrue unjustifiable monopoly profits. Never mind the evidence that economically regulated firms seldom make huge profits. But how valid is this theory of capture?

In the case of economic regulation, the theory is indeed valid in the sense that one version of the theory is desirable and indispensable. To protect an industry from all-out competition by restraining freedom of entry is to prevent the widespread bankruptcies that inevitably accompany unrestricted competition. Indeed, the only standard for determining if there is enough competition in an industry is a combination of constantly falling prices and constantly increasing bankruptcies. As noted earlier, supporters of transportation deregulation routinely apply this standard. A recent and elaborate modification of classical theory, labeled "perfectly contestable markets," seeks to get around the problem of identifying bankruptcies as success by specifying that if, in principle, a new firm could easily enter a market, and could just as easily exit from the industry by recovering all the costs of entry, then "a history of absence of entry . . . and a high concentration index may be signs of virtue, not of vice."[6] Because the theory is based upon the fundamental fallacy of classical economic theology, it makes little sense.*

It bears repeating again and again that bankruptcies are not evidence that inefficient firms are being driven out by more efficient competitors, but are evidence of overcapacity and/or overproduction; even if all firms in a highly competitive market are efficient, some or all firms (or farmers) must fail because the redundancy cannot be sustained. Protection, then, becomes desirable, and it is the schizophrenic basis of economic theory that makes intelligent discussion of the capture theory almost impossible. This can be outlined by comparing three slightly different levels of analysis:

---

*If a hypothetical new entrant could continue in business and make average or better-than-average profits for the foreseeable future, it is unlikely he would sell out for purely economic reasons. The theory, therefore, assumes that supply cannot substantially exceed demand. If supply did substantially exceed demand, the exiting firm could not recoup its initial investment. The economists advancing this theory, however, have been criticized for quite different reasons, associated with their employment by Bell Laboratories. Because the theory provides an approving rationale for less-than-perfect competition, it can be seen as a defense of AT & T.

• An environmentalist is likely to believe that environmental interest groups should play a role in formulating the policies of environmental-protection agencies, and the environmentalist will label such involvement "citizen participation."[7] The affected businesses, of course, will label the involvement a form of regulatory capture, but the environmentalist also will protest if an agency begins to treat the businesses as "friends" instead of "enemies." The currents which swirled about the U.S. Environmental Protection Agency in 1981-83 were examples of this "whose ox is gored?" confusion.[8]

• Business people will condemn regulation or interference, and the U.S. Chamber of Commerce repeatedly advances the general anti-regulation proposition. The firms in each individual industry, however, frequently argue that some form of protection is needed for that industry, but only as an exception to the norm of nonregulation. The argument often includes designation of "villains" guilty of "unfair competition," foreign firms often filling this role. In asking that it be protected while other industries remain unprotected, an industry seeks the best price for what it sells, but the lowest possible price for what it buys.

• As a worker, the individual seeks the job security that is obtainable only through some form of regulation or protection but, as a consumer, the same individual seeks to remove job security from workers in other industries.

Such examples indicate that when a theory is deeply embedded, its slogans are repeated without conscious thought. Upon further consideration, a manager might acknowledge that he needs dependable suppliers of quality materials. Similarly, a worker would admit the desirability of having many consumers (who work in other industries) for the output of his plant.

In another sense, the capture theory appears, at first glance, to raise a problem. Many complain that regulatory agencies are only "revolving doors" that serve the personal or corporate interests of those in regulated industries. Individuals presumably enter the agencies from industry, hoping that if they help industry, more lucrative offers will be made to them when they are ready to leave government. The problem arises because the industries themselves are often the only sources of expertise. It is no solution to appoint as regulators those who know nothing about the industries, for this is analogous to the lack of expertise in conglomerate management. One careful analysis of some regulatory agencies concludes that these forms of corruption or pseudocorruption are not major problems,[9] but recent experience with a form of a "revolving door" indicates why there is a problem at all. A number of individuals who, while in regulatory agencies or on congressional staffs, had worked for deregulation of the airline industry, joined new airlines upon leaving government, even though they had no previous experience in the industry. The problem, then, seems traceable to a competitive environment that virtually compels the firms involved to engage in everything from global espionage to the search for small favors in Washington. Competition is the problem, not regulation per se.

The capture theory ultimately fails because it makes sense only if the consumer sovereignty of the free market makes sense, but all-out competition leads only to a depression. The answer is not to be found in any scheme that seeks to establish or maintain the authority of either producers or consumers to "capture" the other group. Regulation, whatever form it may ultimately take, industry by industry, country by country, and in the world as a whole, must depend upon shared authority. Regulation can work only if there are no wardens and no prisoners. This requires that government itself be no more (but no less) than a partner in, or a member of, any regulatory process in which it must be involved. What should we do?

MOVING INTO PUBLIC WORKS

Two recent books, written by academics who hoped, perhaps, that their conclusions would make sense to the next Democratic president (whenever he or she takes office), seek to straighten out some of the conceptual mess. Robert B. Reich's book was widely advertised as demolishing the accepted explanations for contemporary economic malaise. Readers were urged not to "blame" government deficits, (social) over-regulation, oil prices, or shortages of investment capital.[10] Focusing upon American "decline," Reich concluded that industries should be reorganized (from assembly-line to flexible-system production), and workers retrained to fit the new design. Lester Thurow, vigorously launching a long-overdue attack on the fundamentals of economic theory, concluded that the individualistic basis of the theory is so lacking in merit that the discipline is "in turmoil" and "sinking in a riptide."[11] Essentially, he argued for the adoption of an economic theory based upon social, not individual, preferences. Neither would accept the argument, in this book, that economic regulation must be the point of departure.

If the United States, and many other countries as well, are to cease producing much more than can be sold for production costs, the specter of even higher unemployment immediately arises. Yet recently increasing unemployment in all the advanced countries, and in developing countries as well, has been caused by the global free market itself. If those now laid off were to return to work at their old jobs, a temporary upsurge in production would be followed by an even steeper decline. While American analysts and policy makers hailed the emerging recovery in the spring of 1983, the revised theory in this book suggests that small improvements in economic indicators could not long continue.

To understand the shape of a new beginning, it is necessary to remember once again how America last became prosperous. The last great regulatory scheme occurred due to World War II. Competitors were destroyed, and supplies for consumers were severely limited. Much of the military production was unneeded, although nobody could have known precisely what would be needed. The pattern, however, was one long familiar to farmers. Economic conditions are improved if excess output is destroyed or discarded, because attempts to sell it must ultimately destroy all producers and, when workers lose their jobs, destroy consumers as well. Following the same reasoning, American prosperity was sustained after the war by the equivalent of giveaway programs. While the Marshall Plan and corollary food-aid programs were necessary and justifiable on humanitarian grounds, they also kept Americans at work in producing things that to some extent were surplus in regard to domestic market demand. This approach is easier to manage with respect to food, for obvious reasons: It is virtually impossible to simultaneously sell and give away automobiles. It would appear that public works can do for the economy what World War II did some years ago, provided that the magnitude of the effort is very nearly equivalent, relatively speaking, to that of wartime military production.

The job to be done is huge, but for reasons I will shortly amplify, precise estimates of what must be done are unimportant. All we need do is grasp, to begin with, that the needs constitute something of a job market:

• Fully 45 percent of the country's 557,516 highway bridges are deficient or obsolete.
• The still incompleted interstate highway system is deteriorating to an extent that calls for reconstruction of 2,000 miles per year, with a backlog of 8,000 miles already in existence.
• The rail system is in such a shambles that estimates of repair and renewal costs are impossible to make.
• In 10 of 28 major cities, leaking water systems experience losses of 10 percent or more, and two of the worst cities (New York and Boston) have yet to be surveyed.
• Half of the country's communities have waste-water treatment facilities now operating at full capacity, and other sewer systems have badly deteriorated.

Individual examples of the need appear almost daily:

• In Pittsburgh, U.S. Steel asserts that it pays $1 million each year to detour trucks 26 miles around a major bridge that was closed several years ago for lack of repairs.
• In Albuquerque, sewer lines are crumbling under the streets, and many have become impassable as the city makes bit-by-bit repairs.
• *Texas Monthly* declares that it has counted 1.5 million pot-holes in Houston.
• In New York, broken water mains, subway failures, and the deterioration of other public works facilities have become the norms.*

---

*After this manuscript was completed, a 70-year-old water main burst in Manhattan, flooded an underground power station, causing an electrical fire which left a large commercial area without power for several days. With almost everyone convinced that governments cannot afford such things, nobody stepped forward to advocate large-scale refurbishing of the water system. Indeed, one entrepreneur now advertises, as "a luxurious necessity" ("Don't wait for the next emergency"), a $1,595 "executive leather sofabed" for use when "railroad strikes," "derailments," and "water main breaks" cripple New York. *The New York Times*, Sept. 29, 1983.

The Congressional Budget Office concludes that the country should spend $53.4 billion per year on public-works projects — an increase of about 50 percent over recent expenditure levels.[12] Worrying about the money needed, however, is a waste of everyone's time.

"Rebuilding" is a useful concept, but it falls short of fully describing the tasks we should undertake. Truly giant "mega-projects" are in order if the world, not merely its separate states, regions, or blocs, is to manage the delivery of what is needed (fuel, food, perhaps water) to where it is needed. The most recent U.S. public works project of significant magnitude was the interstate highway system that, as noted above, is now overdue reconstruction. Literally scores of such projects are needed, but the assumption that we cannot afford them discourages many from even thinking about them. Huge logistics and transportation systems, including such components as port complexes (perhaps located offshore) might, for example, develop unbreakable linkages among the continents. There is enough to do to keep the world busy for at least a century.

As substitutes for the most important social institution of the civilized era — war — such projects could, if we were fortunate, replace war as the focus of the most intensive forms of human dedication. Americans should be especially sensitive to the possibility of redefining "greatness" because, as consistently as any society, we label as "great" those who have provided leadership during important, revered, and victorious wars (Washington, Lincoln, Wilson, Franklin Roosevelt). Without the intervention of World War II, Roosevelt might be remembered even now as only a chief executive who failed the test of managing economic recovery. Public, or *civil*, works might enable the world to meet the challenge of inventing non-military prosperity. As George Leonard asserts, "it is doubtful that a momentous surge toward true peacefulness can occur until some great enterprise not involving war becomes clear to us."[13] Public works on a global scale might constitute just such a "great enterprise."

Current policies urge and virtually require that billions upon billions be borrowed and spent on facilities and equipment that may never be used at anywhere near efficient operating levels, because the global free market forces this to occur. We spend on items we do not need, while resolutely insisting that because government projects are wasteful, we cannot afford to borrow and spend on public works. Even worse, the corporate overspending causes a depression, while even wild overspending on public works could not possibly have the same effect. Put another way, it may not be desirable to overspend on public works, but this type of overspending entails far less risk to economic health. Only the commitment to economic theology blinds us to this reality.

When I lived in the nation's capital in the mid-1960s, television-news programs often referred to the "waste" of building and operating Dulles International Airport. It was little used then, and remains underused in the 1980s, in part because policy-makers prefer the convenience for them of nearby Washington National Airport. Yet a recent article in the *Washington Post*, focusing only on the under-use and avoiding broader economic questions, labeled Dulles a "soaring white elephant."[14] Government officials are aware that if a government-built facility stands unused or underused for even a brief time, they will be criticized. But the facilities that stand idle because of the compulsory overbuilding that attends a free market are hardly noticed at all or, when noticed, are ascribed to the poor economic conditions that allegedly caused the idleness.

The fact that the United States produced untold amounts of military hardware for World War II, and then threw much of it away, is a guideline to be observed, if not rigidly followed. There is little need to be cautious about spending on public works, provided that a huge program of that sort is accompanied by economic regulation of the production of things to sell. Indeed, a more precise guideline can be stated. It is far better to be on the verge of rationing some output than it is to have vast industrial overcapacity. Assume for the moment that instead of building a large military force during World War II, the United States had put the same people, and the same funds, into public works. Who can doubt, as noted by the economic historian, Ross Robertson, quoted earlier, that the country and its citizens would have prospered? If America is "in ruins," as careful analysts declare,[15] why the hesitancy about public works?

The answer lies in the evidence presented earlier. Moving beyond Thurow's analysis, economic theory tells us that it is better to build more steel mills, even if the output cannot be sold, than it is to build more bridges; yet the bridges could provide a market for steel mills now idle. Obviously, even some capital which otherwise would go into the unregulated growth of high-tech industries should be diverted into public works. Just as obviously, there is a great need for coordinated planning, considering that public-works expenditures are now managed by 50 states, 3,042 counties, 35,000 general-purpose governments, 15,000 school districts, 26,000 special districts, 2,000 areawide units of government, 200 interstate compacts, and nine multistate regional-development organizations,[16] not to mention all the associated contractors now bidding in competitive processes that will land more and more of them in jail.

A simple but complete reversal is needed. Contrary to what the textbooks and accounting practices tell us, the private sector creates some wealth, but much more waste, while government creates some waste, but could create much more wealth. And the greater the proportion of government borrowing and spending assigned to public works, the better the government ratio of wealth to waste. Consensual decision processes that bring together governments, contractors, labor unions, and citizens need not require a substantial rearrangement of the larger political system, although it is clear that the panoply of antitrust laws and precedents stands as a mighty "impediment" to the emergence of consensual decision processes.[17] Whether for milk in Little Rock, garbage hauling in Minneapolis, or the refurbishing of 250,000 bridges, public-private cartels are in order.

REORGANIZING INDUSTRY

The old New Deal approach offers only the vaguest guidelines, but its central concept remains useful. Similarly, industrial self-regulation (indirectly stimulated by antitrust oversight) was not wholly evil, but the unwillingness or inability to understand how it worked was, and is, a tragedy. For reasons I have outlined elsewhere, and which have to do with the best size of planning groups, the industrial pattern of oligopoly could be transformed into public-private cartel patterns having no more than *five* large firms, or consortia, in each industry.[18] The key is to allow for truly joint planning in everything from research and development to output and pricing. The presumed propensity of large firms to gouge customers — never adequately demonstrated — could be controlled, to whatever extent necessary, by taxes levied upon excess profits. Moreover, prices would not escalate beyond reason, because redundancy costs would be much less. Furthermore, the taxes levied upon consumers for the accumulation of investment capital would be geared to nonredundant expansion. These taxes have been much more economically damaging than those levied by government, and should be drastically reduced.

The most recent U.S. recession, which officially ended in November of 1982, was severe enough to prompt some Washington policymakers to acknowledge that something should be done. The president suggested making international trade a cabinet-level government function (a secretary for competition?), and the Justice Department issued tentative guidelines for permitting competing firms to engage in joint research and development efforts. The announced benchmark would allow collaboration when the partners, taken together, accounted for less than 50 percent of the sales in the industry, and when their efforts would still leave room for at least four-to-six competing joint ventures.[19] The benchmark was ludicrous; using its logic, seven competing groups should have been financed for the purpose of designing alternative approaches to the national space program, or for that matter, the atomic bomb project of World War II. It is often forgotten that such massive duplication as the Justice Department prescribed is made even more wasteful and dysfunctional by virtue of the necessity of competing researchers to conceal reports of their progress (industrial secrets) from each other for as long as possible. Competition in action, then, has the effect of severely inhibiting the free flow of information, even though openness is a declared objective of both economics and science. Secrecy, in turn, encourages espionage and counter-espionage. Obviously, a more sweeping approach is needed, i.e., joint ventures which include all the firms in a given industry.

Such an approach would of course require that conglomerates be dissolved, and would call for the reorganizing of many industries into the design outlined above. The pattern would vary a bit according to the desirability of direct or indirect competition in given industries. If there were five auto makers, for example, consumers could, for the most part, be left with a reasonable number of alternatives from which to choose. Market shares would be relatively stable, however, determined by joint planning among the firms, i.e., legalized dividing of the business. Assuming use of joint research and development and of government-approved safety standards, innovation would be more real than has been the pretense we have been used to, and huge swings in customer preferences would be unlikely. With some of the mystique removed from managerialism, corporate executives obviously would not command the astronomical salaries they have been paid as the unwitting agents of depression.* Competition in many industries would logically become much more indirect; i.e., transportation, communications and banks might well be turned over to regional, or route, monopolies.

Americans, perhaps even more than others in the world, have been trained to believe the opposite, but the costs to them of all-out competition are extremely high. Duplication is an all-embracing phenomenon. As automobile competition becomes more global, for example, every manufacturer must maintain a well-stocked supply line of spare parts which extends to every community in the world in which it sells and services its cars. This is an extraordinarily expensive undertaking. Costs (and, of course, prices) would be substantially lower if automobiles, merely one example of many that could be cited) were more standardized with respect to their basic components. Contrary to conventional wisdom, it is much more likely that competition increases costs and prices instead of reducing them.

In such massive restructuring, governments would be given a voice, but not a fully authoritative one. Their new function would be to restrict competition, not increase it. For a very long time now, antitrust decision making and litigation have been a growth industry, in and out of government, just as merger wars have employed innumerable lawyers, accountants, and financial wizards, all financed by taxpayers and consumers. All of this has had a destabilizing effect beyond comprehension. While enough has been said about mergermania, it can be noted that antitrust settlements are often reached only after years of litigation that stalemate planning until outcomes are known. The costs of seeking to increase competition probably have greatly exceeded any costs incurred in regulating it. By the same token, workers and unions cannot be excluded from planning, yet this would be easier to accomplish than would the dreams of high-tech devotees.

It is well known by now that the myth of high tech holds little promise for displaced workers. While high tech will indeed emerge,

---

*If a business failure cannot properly be ascribed to poor management, it is just as incorrect to ascribe "success" to managerial acumen. It makes no sense to penalize managers for "failing" in an intensely competitive environment, but it is equally inappropriate to shower them with rewards when the environment makes success almost inevitable, as in the years following World War II.

limiting its redundancy will actually save jobs, for these industries are likely to employ fewer people, if more robots, than supporters are yet ready to admit. The basic shift would be from "smokestack," or declining, industries to public works, but this would not be all that great a shift. This would solve yet another problem, for the idea that high-tech and information industries can be sustained without an industrial base is questionable upon its face. The outline thus far is only a beginning, and all the details cannot be filled in here. A shift in thinking, once it influences action, brings to the surface other required changes that cannot be wholly foreseen in advance. Yet the outline remains to be expanded a bit.

CARTELIZING THE WORLD?

The industrial revolution is not all that old, depending upon how any observer dates its origin. If, as many believe, industrialization is in decline in this country, many other countries seek to industrialize for the first time but, as they do, high-tech industries arrive there in search of cheap labor. Indeed, those who proudly labeled themselves "Atari Democrats" as they urged an American commitment to advanced technology, probably were dismayed when the firm of that name moved its production facilities to the Far East. To focus on a transition from one phase of the industrial revolution to another postindustrial phase, however, is to miss the point. The problem is unrestrained competition, whatever the product.

If output regulation is needed, no regulatory scheme can be confined within national boundaries unless imports and exports are completely shut off — i.e., autarky. Protectionism, in the form of quotas and other trade barriers, is a clumsy form of regulation, principally because it is a unilateral action and adopted with the thought that it is yet another temporary remedy for unusual problems. Economists, of course, oppose protectionism in general, since they unwittingly are dedicated to the proposition that all industries should tax and tax (customers) and spend and spend (on facilities and output) their way to a depression. As of 1980, 70 percent of all goods made in the United States were actively competing with goods made elsewhere.[20] This not only indicates great interdependence, but so much duplication of output around the world as to threaten a deep depression. In conditions of global competition, regulation ultimately must take one of two paths. Either there will be global schemes of allocating facilities and output, industry by industry, or there will be a renewal of all-out trade wars as each producing country desperately seeks markets and resources.

The problem is organizational, not ideological. Within any given country, reliance upon free markets leads to overproduction. A colleague (Dorothy Solinger), preparing a book on China's attempt to use free-market approaches, tells me that in some instances, its experience duplicates ours. The Chinese have concluded that "chaotic readjustments" have led to excessive production of such items as fans and bicycles, thereby depleting raw materials while piling up inventories.[21] Along with competition has come the widespread use of deceptive practices. An investigation of 1,109 packages in one city turned up short-weighting in 63 percent of the weighings.[22] Once lying and deception begin, whether in the U.S. or Chinese markets, all producers are swept along. Concluding that too much has been wasted on overproduction and waste, the Chinese have decided to

> collect funds from all state-run enterprises, institutions, government organs and organizations, the army and local governments [because] there has been a shortage of funds for key energy and transportation projects.[23]

If the descriptions are a bit different, the organizational problems are the same. The problems become a bit more visible in a society that does not attempt to distinguish, as we do, between wealth (business) and waste (government). In principle, the Chinese people "own" all enterprises but, when local units are turned loose to compete against each other, only waste emerges. As in Yugoslavia, another country that has attempted "market socialism," disaster is the outcome. If needed public works are to be constructed, resources must be diverted from the wasteful market operations. There even have been indications that the Chinese were reconsidering their decision to permit wider and wider advertising.

The ultimate shape of regulatory schemes, within or among societies, remains to be developed. Concentrating all decision-making authority in a few central agencies might not work in any one country or among all countries. Yet there would seem no alternative to acknowledging that such efforts must begin, within each society and in the world at large. After all, countries routinely admit now that unregulated "overfishing" depletes fish stocks at the fastest possible rate, and that broad multilateral forms of regulation are necessary if such species as the bluefin tuna, for example, are not to become extinct. If we see that any resource is ultimately limited, the unregulated free market quickly depletes it, while putting more of it up for sale than can be used at the time.

When economists turn away from designing prescriptions for free markets in other organizations, and turn their attention to their own organizations, they demonstrate their own commitment to the schizophrenia of their discipline. Their academic salaries depend upon job security (tenure), and they would not welcome unregulated professorial imports in their university societies, even if the immigrants would, by accepting lower salaries, make it possible for students to pay lower prices (tuition).[24] The notion of an unregulated university industry would appall the economists who seek to deregulate all other industries.

A global beginning would acknowledge the permanent requirement for some of the arrangements now believed temporary. If the United States and Japan, for example, agree on how many automobiles, motorcycles, and television sets should be exchanged, this is a form of regulation that, even if numbers vary slightly each year, must become permanent. Logically, the agreement should be extended to include the amount of Japanese-owned facilities in the United States, and vice versa. If, hypothetically, there were only these two countries in the world, it then would be necessary to agree on the total output of such goods in the two countries, and on the division of the market among competing companies. Viewed in this way, much of the importing and exporting would then be seen as unnecessary. After all, the only reason countries now export is to reduce the sales of home-manufactured goods in the importing countries.

One economic principle could turn out to be highly useful in schemes of global regulation. The doctrine of "comparative advantage," correctly interpreted, has considerable merit; each actor, individual or state, should do what she/he/it is best equipped to do at the moment. In an unwittingly immoral way, the doctrine has been applied to human resources by redefining it as "cheap labor," thereby replacing a more justifiable principle: "equal pay for equal work." The substitution has been done for altruistic reasons (lower prices for consumers), but it effectively destroys the correct meaning of the doctrine. The advantage of cheap labor, only a thinly disguised version of slavery, is used to compensate for all sorts of comparative *dis*advantages. The unfortunate result is that all producers turn out the same products, precisely the opposite of the doctrine's meaning.

China and the United States are hardly alone in their common need for huge public-works programs. The needs are indeed enormous everywhere. The world banking crisis is the result of over-lending for cash-producing facilities that, in a world glutted with capacity, by definition, cannot pay off. Even to those who identify public works as waste, the waste of unused plants should be obvious. Indeed, even international giveaway programs for public works are preferable to loans never to be repaid. In this sense, savings take on new meaning. The revenues of government are identical in purpose and operation with savings accumulated in banks and/or by corporations. Allocation of revenues and savings is, across the board, a social function to be accomplished in accordance with a social purpose.

We face a paradox. The goal of affluence, not in the sense of consumer luxury but of comfortable existence, is compatible only with less, not more, production for sale. In this country, as the Great Depression took hold, an outgoing and an incoming president understood this, if only in the clumsiest of intellectual ways. They believed and hoped that the Great Depression was only a temporary interruption, but they agreed that regulation was needed. The agreement did not last long, for the requirement for periodic elections requires that agreements be converted to disagreements for the sake of having political campaigns. The central features of that agreement, however, remain valid today.

GETTING STARTED

Global competition is a market design that transcends ideology, and regulatory schemes must do the same. The first step is to simply reregulate all industries that have been deregulated, this time by recognizing that much horizontal reorganization (merging) is needed. This would indeed be costly in the short run but, at the same time, many of the assets of such industries are worth little in a deregulated market. The corollary requirement is to recognize antitrust laws as a wholly misguided failure. Just as in wars, it is better to simply discard unneeded output than to attempt to find profitable markets for it. On these matters, economics and economists cannot have it both ways.

Virtually everyone proclaims the need for technological innovation, and because everyone constantly searches for the better product, new technologies appear long before existing ones have been fully used. A used plant may turn out goods that must be sold for slightly higher prices than prices for the output of a new plant, but some of the difference is traceable to systems of creative accounting. The decision to adopt the new technology, however, is self-defeating unless accompanied by carefully planned retirement of the facilities then in existence. Demand elasticity does not solve the problem; relatively small price reductions cannot entice enough new customers to buy the output of both old and new facilities.* When new technology does lead to substantial price reductions, as in pocket calculators, unregulated competition soon leads to calamity.

While they are full participants in the globally competitive market, the Japanese have at least acknowledged upon occasion that overcapacity is a very real problem which requires a collaborative solution. When government decided that the chemical industry constituted such a problem, it brought together the 12 ethylene producers to plan a capacity reduction. These firms, along with six ethylene derivative makers, drew up a plan to reorganize the industry into three consortia, each then committed to reducing capacity by 36 percent. Given the Japanese commitment to job security for a substantial portion of the labor force, it was agreed that workers would be sustained through a period of underemployment, since this is accepted as a "welfare aspect of Japanese corporations." Later, they would be shifted to other jobs. Because the planning was only "advisory," although government accepted the plan, the activity

---

*The concept of "creative destruction" has often been used to praise all-out competition as a process of continuously invigorating renewal. Traceable to Joseph Schumpeter, the concept presumably applies to what many would describe as the contemporary changeover from old to new industries. As a proposition easily derived from market theology, "creative destruction" merely seeks to legitimate the devastation which accompanies wasteful overcapacity.

was not considered a violation of Japanese monopoly laws. Essentially, the undertaking is a desirable example of legalized collusion.[25]

Some will respond that any expansion of regulatory schemes ultimately must produce a scarcity, shortage, or even black markets. As with all other attacks on regulation, the critics ignore the inevitable outcomes of competition. When competitors must lie, cheat, deceive, bribe, and engage in other forms of chicanery in order to survive, and when many of them must go to jail for having tried to survive, the "black-market" criticism loses its power. Besides, regulatory schemes need only ensure that production be limited to slightly more than can be sold, so as to avoid the mountains of overproduction that cause a depression. None of this detail need involve massive expansion of government agencies. Moreover, many forms of deregulation have produced the equivalent of black markets.

When banks escalate interest-rate wars for depositors; when conglomerate managers bid up stock prices; when savings are pumped willy-nilly into the stock market; when bell captains capture parts of the tour-bus market by making themselves subcontractors; and when sports owners escalate bidding wars for athletes — these are the same things as black markets. All citizens finance these activities, especially those whose medical, retirement, welfare, and food benefits are reduced for the sake of supporting competitive struggles.

Others doubtless will conclude that the proposals outlined herein would, simply by restricting the number of alternatives available to consumers, infringe upon the liberty of citizens. If the reaction seems valid in one sense, it seems wholly incorrect in a broader sense. The participation of consumers and their interest groups in regulatory processes is more easily accommodated when direct competition is lessened. It might be very appropriate for consumer advocate Nader to serve on the board of directors of an airline operating between New York and Washington, but, if five airlines flew that route, it would be wholly inappropriate for him to be a director for all five firms. The presence of Douglas Fraser, recently retired president of the auto workers' union, on Chrysler's board has presented a problem since he took his seat. In principle, Fraser's function is to assist Chrysler in luring customers away from not only Toyota, but from Ford as well. Those who represent the separate roles of citizens as workers and consumers, therefore, can best perform that function in a collective-planning environment that divides the business, as a substitute for unrestrained competition.

Over time, it would become more obvious that participation in industrial decision making, beginning with an initial product design, is more significant than simply choosing between, say, Oxydol and Wisk at the time of a purchase.

The theory in this book virtually rules out all proposals now under consideration in Washington, and those advanced by other academics as well. For the most part, the proposals boil down to some combination of these: "cut federal deficits," "increase investment in new plants," "retrain workers and managers," "improve management of the money supply," and above all, "make America more competitive." A partial exception is Thurow, who, while supporting some of these clarion calls to action, has concluded that the microeconomic underpinnings of the discipline of economics have badly deteriorated. Stated in a way he might not accept, this means that the quest for consumer sovereignty must end, but so must the renewed effort to achieve producer sovereignty (expressed by supply-side economists), the century-old Marxist crusade for worker sovereignty, and perhaps even the destructive ideal of national sovereignty. Economic theory, essentially identical in all cultures, must turn instead to the concept of voluntary cooperation which many have long espoused but never practiced. This can lead, if we are fortunate, to nonviolent and nonauthoritarian revolution on a global scale. The immediate problem of greatest magnitude lies in those areas about which economists and policy-makers agree, not the trivial matters they debate. If a massive shift in thought and action proves impossible, a tougher question looms ahead: Who will survive the next big war?

NOTES

1. Richard Stennett, *Authority* (New York: Knopf, 1980), p. 15.

2. James MacGregor Burns, *Leadership* (New York: Harper & Row, 1978), p. 1.

3. *Can Regulatory Agencies Protect Consumers?* (Washington, D.C.: American Enterprise Institute for Public Policy Research, 1971), chap. 1.

4. Eugene Bardach and Robert A. Kagan, *Going by the Book: The Problem of Regulatory Unreasonableness* (Philadelphia: Temple University Press, 1982), pp. 44-45.

5. James Q. Wilson, ed., *The Politics of Regulation* (New York: Basic Books, 1981), introduction, p. ix.

6. William J. Baumol, "Contestable Markets: An Uprising in the Theory of Industrial Structure," *The American Economic Review* 72, 1 (March 1982): 3, 14. I thank my colleague, Samuel T. Myers, for bringing this to my attention.

7. This point is made neatly by Wilson, op. cit., pp. ix-x.

8. For the argument that business firms mounted a campaign to "capture" the Federal Trade Commission, see Michael Pertschuk, *Revolt Against Regulation: The Rise and Pause of the Consumer Movement* (Berkeley: University of California Press, 1983).

9. Paul J. Quirk, *Industry Influence on Federal Regulatory Agencies* (Princeton: Princeton University Press, 1981).

10. *New York Times*, Sunday Book Review, May 8, 1983; the book, previously cited, is *The Next American Frontier*.

11. Lester C. Thurow, *Dangerous Currents: The State of Economics* (New York: Random House, 1983), pp. 236-37.

12. *New York Times*, June 4, 1982; July 18, 1982; May 9, 1983. See also Pat Choate and Susan Walter, *America in Ruins: The Decaying Infrastructure* (Durham: Duke University Press, 1983).

13. George B. Leonard, *The Transformation: A Guide to the Inevitable Changes in Humankind* (New York: Delacorte Press, 1972), p. 206.

14. *Washington Post*, Jan. 16, 1983.

15. Choate and Walter, op. cit.

16. *New York Times*, July 18, 1982.

17. Andrew F. Popper, "The Antitrust System: An Impediment to the Development of Negotiation Models," *The American University Law Review*, 32 (Winter 1983): 279-82.

18. See my *An End to Hierarchy & Competition: Administration in the Post-Affluent World*, 2d ed. (New York and London: Franklin Watts, New Viewpoints, 1981), esp. chap. 1. Briefly, consensus decisions, without voting, work best in five-member groups. If more than five individuals or organizations must be involved, the larger group should be divided into smaller groups, which then are linked together for consensus-producing purposes.

19. See *New York Times*, May 11, 1983.

20. Reich, op. cit., p. 121.

21. *Beijing People's Daily*, May 3, 1980, p. 2.

22. Ibid., April 25, 1980, p. 3.

23. Foreign Broadcast Information Service, December 23, 1982.

24. This elaborates a point in Thurow, op. cit., p. 192.

25. *New York Times*, May 18, 1983.

About the Author

FREDERICK C. THAYER is, for 1983-84, a visiting faculty member at the Washington Public Affairs Center of the University of Southern California. Since 1969, he has been on the faculty of the Graduate School of Public & International Affairs of the University of Pittsburgh.

Dr. Thayer has published widely on organization theory and its linkages with economic and political theory and practice, and on air transport policy. His articles have appeared in such journals as *The Annals of the American Academy of Political and Social Science, Administration and Society*, and *Public Administration Review*. His most recent book was *An End to Hierarchy & Competition: Administration in the Post-Affluent World*.

Dr. Thayer holds a B.S. from the U.S. Military Academy at West Point, an M.A. from The Ohio State University, and a Ph.D. from the Graduate School of International Studies of The University of Denver.